Saved

By
EDWARD BOND

**A Full-Length Play
For Seven Men
and
Three Women**

THE DRAMATIC PUBLISHING COMPANY

SAVED

This play was first staged in November 1965 at the Royal Court Theatre before members of the English Stage Society, after a license for public performance of the play as it stands had been refused. It quickly became the subject of fierce debate and has passed into the international repertoire of the modern theatre.

"In his play of marvellous observed dialogue and first-rate dramatic form, Edward Bond places his act of violence in the first half, as is done in *Macbeth, Julius Caesar,* etc. Unfortunately the extreme horror of this scene, though no more lurid than many an accustomed fact to which English railway toilets give testimony, has run away with most dramatic criticism and blinded it to the rare qualities shown in the rest of the play, which from time to time achieves astonishing heights of dramatic prowess . . . *Saved* is not for children but it is for grown-ups, and the grown-ups of this country should have the courage to look at it . . . "

Sir Laurence Olivier in a letter to The Observer

"Mr. Bond is out to rub noses in the fact that the real new poor are the old poor plus television, sinking deeper in a form of poverty we do not yet recognize — poverty of culture . . ."

Ronald Bryden in the New Statesman

AUTHOR'S NOTE

Saved is almost irresponsibly optimistic. Len, the chief character, is naturally good, in spite of his upbringing and environment, and he remains good in spite of the pressures of the play. But he is not wholly good or easily good because then his goodness would be meaningless, at least for himself. His faults are partly brought home to him by his ambivalence at the death of the baby and his morbid fascination with it afterwards.

It is true that at the end of the play Len does not know what he will do next, but he never has done. On the other hand, he has created the chance of a friendship with the father, and he has been chastened but he has not lost his resilience (he mends the chair). The play ends in a silent social stalemate, but if the spectator thinks this is pessimistic that is because he has not learned to clutch at straws. Clutching at straws is the only realistic thing to do. The alternative, apart from the self-indulgence of pessimism, is a fatuous optimism based on superficiality of both feeling and observation. The gesture of turning the other cheek is often the gesture of refusing to look facts in the face — but this is not true of Len. He lives with people at their worst and most hopeless (that is the point of the final scene) and does not turn away from them. I cannot imagine an optimism more tenacious, disciplined or honest than his.

Curiously, most theatre critics would say that for the play to be optimistic Len should have run away. Fifty years ago when, the same critics would probably say, moral standards were higher, they would have praised him for the loyalty and devotion with which he stuck to his post.

By not playing his traditional role in the tragic Oedipus pattern of the play, Len turns it into what is formally a comedy. The first scene is built on the young man's sexual insecurity — he

5

either invents interruptions himself or is interrupted by the old man. Len has to challenge him, and get him out of the house, before he can continue. Later he helps the old man's wife, and this is given a sexual interpretation by the onlookers. Later still the old man finds him with his wife in a more obviously sexual situation. The Oedipus outcome should be a row and death. There *is* a row, and even a struggle with a knife — but Len persists in trying to help. The next scene starts with him stretched on the floor with a knife in his hand, and the old man comes in dressed as a ghost — but neither of them is dead. They talk, and for once in the play someone apart from Len is as honest and friendly as it is possible for him to be. The old man can only give a widow's mite, but in the context it is a victory — and a *shared* victory. It is trivial to talk of defeat in this context. The only sensible object in defeating an enemy is to make him your friend. That happens in this play, although in fact most social and personal problems are solved by alienation or killing.

I also shut out Len from the relation between Pam and Fred because (among other things) this let me explore the Oedipus atmosphere at other stages. In particular, the murder of the baby shows the Oedipus, atavistic fury fully unleashed. The scene is typical of what some people do when they act without restraint, and is not true just of these particular people and this particular occasion. Everyone knows of worse happenings. This sort of fury is what is kept under painful control by other people in the play, and that partly accounts for the corruption of their lives.

Clearly the stoning to death of a baby in a London park is a typical English understatement. Compared to the "strategic" bombing of German towns it is a negligible atrocity, compared to the cultural and emotional deprivation of most of our children its consequences are insignificant.

Like most people I am a pessimist by experience, but an

6

optimist by nature, and I have no doubt that I shall go on being true to my nature. Experience is depressing, and it would be a mistake to be willing to learn from it.

I did not write the play only as an Oedipus comedy. Other things in it — such as the social comment — are more important, but I have not described them in detail here because they are more obvious.

There is, however, a final matter. If we are to improve people's behavior we must first increase their moral understanding, and this means teaching morality to children in a way that they find convincing. Although I suppose that most English people do not consciously disbelieve in the existence of God, not more than a few hundred of them fully believe in his existence. Yet almost all the morality taught to our children is grounded in religion. This in itself makes children morally bewildered — religion has nothing to do with their parents' personal lives, or our economic, industrial and political life, and is contrary to the science and rationalism they are taught at other times. For them religion discredits the morality it is meant to support.

Their problems in studying science and art are those of understanding — but in a religious morality it is one of believing. Most children, as they grow older, cannot believe in religion. We no longer believe in it ourselves, and it is therefore foolish to teach children to do so. The result is that they grow up morally illiterate, and cannot understand, because they have not been properly taught, the nature of a moral consideration or the value of disinterested morals at all.

This is not always noticed because we use words that still have moral connotations, but these are being lost and soon we could well be morally bankrupt. The prevalent morality can be described as opportunist prudentialism, and it is usually expressed with a nauseous sentimentality that I have avoided in

7

this play because it sounds like parody.

There will always be some people sophisticated enough to do the mental gymnastics needed to reconcile science and religion. But the mass of people will never be able to do this, and as we live in an industrial society they will be educated in the scientific tradition. This means that in future religion will never be more than the opium of the intellectuals.

For several reasons morals cannot be slapped on superficially as a social lubricant. They must share a common basis with social organization and be consistent with accepted knowledge. You cannot, that is, "Have the fruit without the root." Most people, when they think about this, ask only what *they* believe, or perhaps what has been revealed to them. But if they are interested in the welfare of others they should ask "what is it possible for most people to believe?" And that means teaching, oddly enough, moral scepticism and analysis, and not faith.

SAVED was first presented by the English Stage Company at the Royal Court Theatre, London, on November 3, 1965, with the following cast:

LEN, twenty-one. Tall, slim, firm, bony. Big hands. High, sharp cheekbones. Pleasant pale complexion – not ashen. Blue eyes, thick fair hair a bit oily, brushed sideways from a parting. Prominent feet.

John Castle

FRED, twenty-one. Blond, very curly hair. Medium height. Well-shaped, steady, powerful body. Light tenor voice.

Tony Selby

HARRY, sixty-eight. Tall. Long thin arms. Long hands. Heavy, bony head with large eye-sockets and small eyes. Loose chin. Gray.

Richard Butler

PETE, twenty-five. Tallish. Well-built, red-faced. Makes very few gestures. Soft hair that tends to stick up lightly.

Ronald Pickup

COLIN, eighteen. Shortish. A bit thin. Loose (but not big) mouth. Shiny ears, curved featureless face. A few spots. Shouts to make himself heard.

Dennis Waterman

MIKE, twenty. Tall. Well-built. Strong, easy, emphatic movements. Pleasant. Dark hair.

John Bull

BARRY, twenty. A little below medium height. Fat.

William Stewart

PAM, twenty-three. Thin, sharp-busted. Heavy, nodal hips. Dark hair. Long narrow face. Pale eyes. Small mouth. Looks tall from a distance, but is shorter than she looks.

Barbara Ferris

MARY, fifty-three. Shortish. Round heavy shoulders. Big buttocks. Bulky breasts, lifeless but still high. Big thighs and little ankles. Curled gray hair that looks as if it is in a hair-net. Homely.

Gwen Nelson

LIZ, exactly as she sounds.   *Alison Frazer*

SCENE ONE

The living room. The front and the two side walls make a triangle
  that slopes to a door back center.
Furniture: Table down right, sofa left, television set left front,
  armchair up right center, two chairs close to the table.
Empty.
The door opens. LEN comes in. He goes straight out again.

PAM (offstage). In there.

(LEN comes in. He goes down to the sofa. He stares at it.)

PAM (offstage). All right?

(Pause. PAM comes in.)

LEN. This ain' the bedroom.
PAM. Bed ain' made.
LEN. Oo's bothered?
PAM. It's awful. 'Ere's nice.
LEN. Suit yourself. Yer don't mind if I take me shoes off?
  (He kicks them off.) No one 'ome?
PAM. No.
LEN. Live on yer tod?
PAM. No.
LEN. Oh. (Pause. He sits back on the couch.) Yer all right?
  Come over 'ere.

11

PAM. In a minit.

LEN. Wass yer name?

PAM. Yer ain' arf nosey.

LEN. Somethin' up?

PAM. Can't I blow me nose? (She puts her hanky back in her bag and puts it on the table.) Better. (She sits on the couch.)

LEN. Wass yer name?

PAM. Wass yourn?

LEN. Len.

PAM. Pam.

LEN. Oh. (He feels the couch behind with his hand.) This big enough?

PAM. What yer want? Bligh!

LEN. Don't wan' a push yer off. Shove that cushion up.

PAM. 'Ang on.

LEN. 'Ow often yer done this?

PAM. Don't be nosey.

LEN. Take yer shoes off.

PAM. In a minit.

LEN. Can yer move yer — thass better.

PAM. Yer d'narf fidget.

LEN. I'm okay now.

PAM. Ow!

LEN. D'yer 'ave the light on?

PAM. Suit yourself.

LEN. I ain' fussy.

PAM. Ow!

LEN. Can yer shut them curtains? (PAM goes left to the curtains.) Yer got a fair ol' arse.

PAM. Like your mug.

LEN. Know somethin'? — I ain' touched a tart for weeks.

PAM. Don't know what yer missin'.

LEN. Don't I? (PAM sits on the couch, on the edge. LEN pulls her closer and takes off her shoes.) Lucky.

PAM. What?

LEN. Bumpin' in t'you.
PAM. Yeh.
LEN. Yer don't mind me?
PAM. No.
LEN. Sure?
PAM. Yer wan'a get on with it.
LEN. Give us a shout if I do somethin' yer don't reckon.
PAM. Bligh! Yer ain' better 'ave.
LEN. I could go for you. Know that? (Pause.) This is the
  life.
PAM. Ow!
LEN. Sh! Keep quiet now.
PAM. Oi!
LEN. Sh!
PAM. Yer told me t'shout!

(The door opens. HARRY comes in. He goes straight out
  again.)

LEN (lifts his head). 'Ere!
PAM. What?
LEN. Oo's that?
PAM. Ol' man.
LEN (sits). Whass 'e want?
PAM. That cushion's stickin' in me back.
LEN. I thought yer reckon yer was on yer tod?
PAM. 'E's late for work.
LEN. Oh. Why?
PAM. Why?
LEN. Yeh.
PAM. I don't know.
LEN. Reckon 'e saw?
PAM. Shouldn't be surprised.
LEN. Will 'e be long?
PAM. Don't arst me.

LEN. Oh. Well. (They lie down again. Slight pause. LEN lifts his head.) 'Ear that?

PAM. No.

LEN. I 'eard somethin'. (He goes to the door. He listens. He goes back to the couch and sits on the end.)

PAM. Well?

LEN. Better 'ang on.

PAM. Why?

LEN. Better 'ad.

PAM. Think yer'll last?

LEN. Not if yer lie around like that.

PAM. Like what?

LEN. Sit up.

PAM. I juss got right.

LEN. More'n I 'ave. Chriss. (He feels in his pocket.) You smoke?

PAM. In me bag.

LEN. Where's yer bag? (PAM nods at the table. LEN goes to the bag and takes out a cigarette. He lights it. He starts putting the cigarettes back.) Oh, sorry. (He holds the packet out to her.)

PAM. No, thanks. (LEN puts the cigarettes away. He sits on the edge of the couch. Pause. He taps his foot three or four times.)

LEN. Wass 'is caper?

PAM. Wan'a cup a tea?

LEN. After.

PAM. 'E won't be long.

LEN. 'Adn't better. 'Ave a puff?

PAM. No.

LEN. Do yer dress up.

PAM. Sorry.

LEN. Yer never know 'oo's poppin' in. (He goes to the door and opens it.)

PAM. You off?

LEN. I could'a swore I 'eard 'eavy breathin'.

PAM. Thass you.

LEN. 'Oo else yer got knockin' about? Yer ain't stuffed yer grannie under the sofa?

PAM. She's dead.

LEN. 'Ard luck. — Wass 'is caper? (He sits on a chair.) My blinkin' luck. (He stands and walks.) 'E'll be late, won't 'e! I 'ope they dock 'is bloody packet. (He listens by the door.) Not a twitter.

PAM. 'E ain' bin out the back yet.

LEN. The ol' twit. (PAM laughs.) Wass the joke?

PAM. You.

LEN (amused). Yeh. Me. Ha! 'E's a right ol' twit, ain' 'e! 'Ere, can I stay the night?

PAM. Ain' yer got nowhere?

LEN. Yeh! — Well?

PAM. No.

LEN. Yer're the loser. — Sure's 'e's goin'? — Why can't I?

PAM. Blight! I only juss met yer.

LEN. Suppose 'e's stoppin' 'ome? Got a cold or somethin'. I'd do me nut! — Yer'd enjoy it.

PAM. Big 'ead.

LEN. 'Ow many blokes yer 'ad this week?

PAM. We ain't finished Monday yet!

LEN. We'll take that into consideration.

PAM. Saucy bugger! (They laugh.) 'Ow many times yer 'ad it this week?

LEN. I told yer once! 'Ow many blokes yer 'ad all told? (They laugh.)

PAM. What about you an' girls?

LEN. Can't count over sixty. (They laugh.)

PAM. Sh!

LEN. 'E'll 'ear. — Oi, tell us!

PAM. 'Ow many times yer done it in one night? (They laugh.)

LEN. Why did the woman with three tits shoot 'erself?

PAM. Eh?

LEN. She only 'ad two nipples. (They laugh.)

PAM. I don't get it. (She laughs.) What did the midwife say to the nun?

LEN. Don't know. (She whispers in his ear. They laugh.) You're great! What about the woman with three tits 'oo 'ad quads?

PAM. Eh?

LEN. That'll teach 'er t'sleep with siamese twins! (They laugh. He whispers in her ear.)

PAM. Yer ought a be locked up!

LEN. That's a feedin' problem!

PAM. Sh — thass the back door. 'E's bin out the lav.

LEN. Less give 'im a thrill. (He jumps noisily on the couch.) Cor — blimey!

PAM. You're terrible! (He takes some sweets from her bag.) They're my sweets.

LEN. Less 'ave a choose. (Loudly.) 'Ow's that for size?

PAM. What yer shoutin'?

LEN (he puts a sweet in her mouth). Go easy! Yer wanna make it last! (She laughs. He bites a sweet in half and looks at it.) Oo, yer got a lovely little soft centre. (Aside to PAM.) First time I seen choclit round it! (He jumps on the sofa.)

PAM (shrill). Yer awful!

LEN. That still 'ard?

PAM (laughs). Leave off!

LEN. Come on, there's plenty more where that come from. (He puts a sweet in her mouth.)

PAM (splutters). Can't take no more!

LEN. Yeh — open it. Yer can do a bit more!

PAM. Ow!

LEN. Oorr lovely! (He tickles her. She chokes.) This'll put 'airs on yer chest! (They try to laugh quietly.)

(The door opens. HARRY puts his head in. He goes out. He

shuts the door. LEN calls.)

LEN. 'Ave a toffee!

PAM. Oo-oo 'ave a toffee!

LEN. Tried that mint with the 'ole in it?

PAM. 'Ave a toffee!

LEN. What about the ol' dolly mixture? — Will 'e give yer a
ruckin'?

PAM. Ain' got the nerve.

LEN (calls). Nosey ol' gander! (They laugh.) See 'is tongue
'angin' out?

PAM. 'E's fetchin' 'is dinner-box out the kitchen.

LEN (calls). Don't work too 'ard, mate!

PAM. Lay off, or 'e'll stay in out a spite.

LEN (calls). Take a toffee for tea break, Dad! — I'd like'a sleep
round 'ere. Yer'd be lovely an' warm in the mornin'.

PAM. Yer're juss greedy!

LEN. I give yer 'alf the sweets!

PAM. I paid. Anyway, Mum'll be back.

LEN. Oh. That the front door?

PAM. Yeh. (She goes to the curtains.) 'E's off.

LEN. Didn't take long.

PAM. I tol' yer.

LEN. Better be worth waitin' for.

PAM. Up to you, ain' it!

LEN. Thass all right then. (She comes to the sofa and starts
to undo his belt.) This is the life.

SCENE TWO

Park.
PAM and LEN in a rowing boat. Otherwise stage bare.

LEN. Cold?
PAM. No.
LEN. Still pecky?
PAM. Yeh.
LEN. There's a bit'a choclit left. 'Ere.
PAM. No.
LEN. Go on.
PAM. Ta.
LEN. Thass yer lot.
PAM. Why?
LEN. No more. (Silence.) I still ain' paid me rent this week.
PAM. Me mum won't reckon that.
LEN. Ain' got round to it.
PAM. Surprised she ain' said. (Slight pause.)
LEN. She ever let on?
PAM. 'Bout us?
LEN. Yeh.
PAM. No.
LEN. She don't mind?
PAM. Don't 'ave to. Your money comes in 'andy. (Silence.)
LEN. She reckon me, yer reckon?
PAM. Never arst.
LEN. Thought she might'a said.
PAM. Never listen.
LEN. Oh.
PAM. Yer ain't spent it?
LEN. 'Er rent?
PAM. Yeh.

LEN. Nah!

PAM. Juss wondered.

LEN. Don' yer truss me?

PAM. I'm goin' a knit yer a jumper.

LEN. For me?

PAM. I ain' very quick.

LEN. Can't say I noticed.

PAM. Yer'll 'ave t'buy the wool.

LEN. Knew there'd be a catch.

PAM. I got a smashin' pattern.

LEN. You worried about that rent?

PAM. I 'ad it give us.

LEN. Yer 'adn't better be one of them naggers.

PAM. What color's best?

LEN. Thass about one thing your ol' girl *don't* do.

PAM. What?

LEN. Nag 'er ol' man.

PAM. What's yer best color?

LEN. They all suit me.

PAM. I like a red. Or a blue.

LEN. Anythin' bright. (Slight pause.)

PAM. I 'ave t' 'ave an easy pattern.

LEN. Will it be ready for the 'oneymoon?

PAM. We ain' 'avin' 'oneymoon.

LEN. 'Oo's payin'?

PAM. You.

LEN. I can see I'll 'ave t' watch out. (Pause.)

PAM. Whass the time?

LEN. Don't know.

PAM. Gettin' on.

LEN. Shouldn't wonder.

PAM. Where's the choclit?

LEN. Yer 'ad it all.

PAM. Oh.

LEN. Sorry.

PAM. There weren't much.

LEN. I'll get some when we go in.

PAM. I 'ad a blinkin' great dinner.

LEN. I reckon yer got a kid on the way.

PAM. I ain'.

LEN. Never know yer luck.

PAM. Yer'll 'ave t' get up early in the mornin' t' catch me.

LEN. Done me best.

PAM. Yer got a dirty mind. (Slight pause.)

LEN. I'm 'andy with me 'ands. Yer know, fix up the ol' dec-
    oratin' lark and knock up a few things. Yeh. We'll 'ave a
    fair little place. I ain' livin' in no blinkin' sty.

PAM. Sounds all right.

LEN. Easy t' kep swep' out an' that. Yer'll be all right.

PAM. I'd better. (He puts his head in her lap. There is a slight
    pause.)

LEN. 'S great 'ere. (Pause.) Pam.

PAM. What?

LEN. Why did yer pick me up like that?

PAM. Why?

LEN. Yeh.

PAM. Sorry then?

LEN. Tell us.

PAM. 'Ow many girls you 'ad?

LEN. No, I tol' yer my life.

PAM. 'Old on.

LEN. What?

PAM. Yer got a spot.

LEN. Where?

PAM. 'Old still.

LEN. Is it big?

PAM. 'Old still.

LEN. Go easy!

PAM. Got it!

LEN. Ow! (PAM bursts a spot on his neck.)

PAM. Give us yer 'anky.

LEN. Yer got it?

PAM. Yeh.

LEN. Ow! It d'narf 'urt. (He gives her his handkerchief. She dips her hand in the water and dries it on the handkerchief. She gives it back to him.)

PAM. Yer wan'a wash sometimes.

LEN. Cheeky cow. (Slight pause. They are both lying down.) Yer wouldn't go back with any ol' sod?

PAM. You are rotten.

LEN. I'm sorry. Pam?

PAM. You're 'urtin' me leg.

LEN. I'm sorry.

PAM. No.

LEN. When yer goin' a start me jumper?

PAM (still annoyed). Why d'yer 'ave t' say that?

LEN. Tell us about me jumper.

PAM. Ain' got no wool.

LEN. I'll get it t'morra. An' we'll start lookin' for a place t'morra.

PAM. No places round 'ere.

LEN. Move out a bit. It's better out.

PAM. Yer'll be lucky.

LEN. Bin lucky with you. (His head is in her lap. He twists so that he can put his arms around her.) Ain' I bin lucky with you?

PAM. Yer don't deserve it.

LEN. I said I'm sorry — I won't arst no more. It's me good looks done it.

PAM. It *was* you. It weren't no one else.

LEN. Less go t'bed early t'night.

PAM. If yer go t'bed much earlier it won't be worth gettin' up.

LEN. Lovely. 'Ow about a sing-song.

PAM. No.

LEN (sings).
>Be kind to yer four-footed friends
>That duck may be somebody's brother
>Yer may think that this is the end
>Well it is.

(Slight pause.)   They must a forgot us.   We bin 'ere 'ours.
PAM. Do the rest.
LEN.   Some mothers!   (Pause.)   Livin' like that must'a got yer down.
PAM. Used to it.
LEN. They ought to be shot.
PAM. Why?
LEN. Don't it ever worry yer?
PAM. 'Ow?
LEN. Supposed you turned out like that?
PAM. No.
LEN. 'Ow'd it start?
PAM. Never arst.
LEN. No one said?
PAM. Never listen. It's their life.
LEN. But –
PAM.   Yer can't do nothin', yer know.   No one'll thank yer.
LEN. 'Ow long's it bin goin' on?
PAM.   Longer'n I know. (Pause. He sits and leans toward her.)
LEN. Must a bin bloody rotten when yer was a kid.
PAM.   Never know'd no difference. They 'ad a boy in the war.
LEN. Theirs?
PAM. Yeh.
LEN. I ain't seen 'im.
PAM. Dead.
LEN. Oh.
PAM. A bomb in a park.
LEN. That what made 'em go funny?
PAM. No. I come after.
LEN. What a life.

PAM. I 'ad me moments.

LEN. I won't turn out like that. I wouldn't arst yer if I didn't know better'n that. That sorty of carry-on ain' fair.

PAM. I know.

LEN. We'll get on all right. I wonder it never sent yer off yer nut.

PAM. Yer don't notice.

LEN. It won't be long now. Why don't yer blow up an' knock their 'eads t'gether?

PAM (shrugs). I 'ope I never see 'em again. Thass all. (Slight pause. LEN looks around.)

LEN. I ain' got a decent jumper. (Pause.) 'Ow'd they manage?

PAM. When?

LEN. They write notes or somethin'?

PAM. No.

LEN. 'Ow's that?

PAM. No need.

LEN. They must.

PAM. No.

LEN. Why?

PAM. Nothin' t' say. 'E puts 'er money over the fire every Friday, an' thass all there is. Talk about somethin' else.

LEN. Whass she say about 'im?

PAM. Nothin'.

LEN. But —

PAM. She never mentions 'im an' 'e never mentions 'er. I don' wanna talk about it.

LEN. They never mention each other?

PAM. I never 'eard 'em.

LEN. Not once?

PAM. *No*!

LEN. It's wet down 'ere. (Pause.) I ain' livin' with me in-laws, thass a fact.

FRED (offstage). Four!

LEN. I never got yer placed till I saw yer ol' people.

PAM. I never chose 'em!

LEN. I never meant that! —

PAM. Don't know why yer wan'a keep on about 'em!

LEN. — I never try an' get at yer!

(FRED comes on down right. His back is to the audience.)

FRED. Number-four-bang-on-the-door!

PAM. Thass us.

FRED. Less 'ave yer!

LEN. Less stay out!

PAM. Why?

FRED. Oi!

PAM (to LEN). Come on.

LEN. We're a pirate ship.

FRED (taking the micky). You devil!

PAM. Yer'll 'ave t' pay.

LEN. Come an' get us!

FRED. Wass up, darlin'? 'As 'e got 'is rudder stuck?

PAM (to LEN). I'm 'ungry.

LEN. Why didn't yer say? (He starts to pull in. FRED moves toward them as the boat comes in.)

FRED. Lovely. 'Elp 'im, darlin'. Thass lovely. She 'andles that like a duchess 'andles a navvy's pick.

LEN. All right?

FRED. Lovely. (He leans out and jerks the boat in. PAM stands awkwardly.)

LEN. Steady.

FRED. 'Old tight, darlin'. (He lifts her out.) Yer wanna watch Captain Blood there. Very nice.

LEN. Okay?

PAM. Ta.

FRED. Very 'ow's yer father.

LEN (stepping out). Muddy.

PAM (to LEN). I enjoyed that.

FRED. Same 'ere.

LEN. We'll do it again.

FRED. Any time.

PAM (to LEN). Got everythin'?

FRED (to PAM). You 'ave.

LEN (clowning). Watch it!

FRED. 'Oo's bin 'aving a bash on me duckboards?

PAM (to LEN). Less 'ave me bag.

FRED. Bashin's extra.

PAM. Yer wanna get yerself a job.

FRED. I got one.

PAM. 'Irin' out boats!

FRED. I'd rather 'ire you out, darlin'.

LEN (joking). Watch it!

PAM (to LEN). Ready?

LEN. Yeh. (LEN and PAM start to go right.)

FRED. Why, you got a job for us? I wouldn't mind a bit a grind for you.

PAM. Yer'll 'ave t' join the union.

FRED. I'm in, love. Paid up.

LEN (joking). Yer'll be in the splash in a minute. (LEN and PAM go out left.)

FRED (to himself). Right up. Like you, darlin'.

SCENE THREE

Park. Bare stage.

PETE, BARRY, MIKE, COLIN. PETE wears a brown suit and suede shoes. The jacket is short in the seat and tight on the shoulders. His tie is black. The others wear jeans and shirts.

MIKE. What time they bury the bugger?

PETE. Couldn't tell yer.

COLIN. Don' yer wan'a go?

PETE. Leave off! 'Oo's goin' a make me time up?

COLIN. Why yer goin' then?

PETE. The ol' lady'll ruck if I don't.

MIKE. Yeh, they reckon anythin' like this.

COLIN. Blinkin' morbid.

MIKE. Looks lovely in a black tie, don' 'e! (They laugh.)

PETE. What a carry on! 'E come runnin' round be'ind the bus. Only a nipper. Like a flash I thought right yer nasty bastard. Only ten or twelve. I jumps right down on me revver an' bang I got 'im on me off-side an' 'e shoots right out under this lorry comin' straight on.

MIKE. Crunch.

COLIN. Blood all over the shop.

MIKE. The fall a the Roman Empire.

PETE. This lorry was doin' a ton in a built-up street.

BARRY. Garn! Yer never seen 'im.

PETE. No?

BARRY. 'It 'im before yer knew 'e was comin'.

PETE (lighting his pipe). Think I can't drive?

COLIN. What a giggle, though.

MIKE. Accidents is legal.

COLIN. Can't touch yer.

PETE. This coroner twit says 'e's sorry for troublin' me.

MIKE. The law thanks 'im for 'is 'elp.

PETE. They paid me for comin'.

MIKE. An' the nip's mother reckons 'e ain' got a blame 'isself.

COLIN. She'll turn up at the funeral.

PETE. Rraammmmmmmmmmm!

COLIN. Bad for the body work.

MIKE. Can't yer claim insurance?

PETE. No.

MIKE. Choked!

COLIN. Ruined 'is paint work.

BARRY. 'E's 'avin' yer on!

MIKE. Yer creep.

COLIN. Yer big creep.

PETE. Let 'im alone. 'E don't know no better.

COLIN. 'E don't know nothin'.

MIKE. Big stingy creep.

COLIN. Yer wouldn't 'ave the guts.

BARRY. No guts?

MIKE. Yeh.

BARRY. Me?

COLIN. Not yer grannie.

BARRY. I done blokes in.

MIKE. 'Ere we go.

BARRY. More'n you 'ad 'ot dinners. In the jungle. Shootin'
    up the yeller-niggers. An' cut 'em up after with the ol' pig-
    sticker. Yeh. (MIKE hoots.)

COLIN. Do leave off!

BARRY. You lot wouldn't know a stiff if it sat up and shook
    'ands with yer!

MIKE. Aa! Shootin' up the yeller-nigs!

COLIN. Sounds like brothers a your'n.

BARRY. Get stuffed!

PETE (to them all). Chuck it, eh?

COLIN. Yeller-niggers! My life! What yer scratchin'?

MIKE. 'E's got a dose.

PETE. Ain' surprisin'.

COLIN. Ain' it dropped off yet?

MIKE. Tied on with a ol' johnny.

COLIN. It's 'is girl.

MIKE. 'Is what?

PETE. Gunged-up ol' boot.

COLIN. 'E knocked it off in the back a 'is car last night –

MIKE. 'Is what?

PETE. Pile a ol' scrap.

MIKE. Ought a be put off the road.

COLIN. 'E was knockin' it off in the back an' –

MIKE. I 'eard.

PETE. What?

MIKE. The back bumper fell off.

PETE. Yeh?

COLIN. I's a fact!

PETE. My life!

MIKE. An' what she say?

COLIN. Yer juss drop somethin'.

BARRY. Bollocks! (He laughs at himself.)

MIKE. Yeh!

COLIN. 'Aving trouble with yer 'orn?

BARRY. It weren't no bumper! Me fog lamp come off.

MIKE. 'Is fog lamp! (They roar with laughter.)

COLIN. I knew somethin' come off!

MIKE. Flippin' fog lamp!

PETE. Thass what she calls it!

COLIN. Wonder it weren't 'is engine come out.

BARRY. Better'n nothin'.

MIKE. Yer couldn't knock someone down with that!

PETE. It'd come t' a stop.

MIKE. Shootin' up the yeller-niggers!

BARRY. Yeh, yer ain' lived!

(LEN comes on down right.)

PETE. Me mum's got a dirty great wreath.

MIKE. Yeh!

COLIN. Give somethin' for it?

PETE. I ain' a 'ippocrit.

COLIN. Oi — whass-yer-name!

LEN. Eh?

COLIN. It's — Lenny, ain' it?

LEN. Yeh. — Oh! 'Ow's it goin', admiral?

COLIN. 'Ow's yerself?

LEN. Not so dodgy. Long time.

COLIN. Me and 'im was t'school t'gether.
MIKE. Yeh?
COLIN. What yer bin doin'?
BARRY. Reform school?
MIKE. Don't 'e show yer up!
COLIN. Take no notice. Creep! — Workin'?
LEN. Worse luck.
COLIN. I couldn't place yer for a minute. (Slight pause.) Yeh.
LEN. Yer ain' changed much.
BARRY. What yer doin' now?
LEN. Waitin'.
MIKE. I — I!
COLIN. It was in the park, yer 'onor!
MIKE. This girl come up t'me.
COLIN. An' drags me in the bushes.
BARRY. Yer 'onor. (He laughs.)
COLIN. I knew she was thirteen.
MIKE. But she twisted me arm.
COLIN. An' 'er ol' dad'd been bashin' it off for years.
BARRY. Yer 'onor. (He laughs.)
COLIN. Twisted yer what?
MIKE. Never know yer luck!
COLIN. Married?
LEN. Gettin' ready.
BARRY. 'Oo with?
LEN. We're waitin' —
COLIN. Pull the other one!
MIKE. What for?
PETE. Till she drops 'er nipper.
COLIN. Else it looks bad goin' up the aisle.
MIKE. She can 'ide it be'ind 'er flowers.
BARRY. Is that what they carry 'em for?
COLIN. We live an' learn.
MIKE. Takes all sorts.

(MARY comes on up right.)

LEN. Thass us.
COLIN. *That*? (LEN goes to MARY.)
PETE. One man's meat.
MIKE. More like scrag-end.
BARRY. Bit past it, ain' she?
PETE. She's still got the regulation 'oles.
MIKE. Experience 'elps. Yer get a surprise sometimes.
LEN (to MARY). Less give yer a 'and.
MARY. Whew! Ta. (She gives LEN the shopping bag.)
LEN. Okay?
MARY. I was juss goin' ter drop 'em.
MIKE. 'Ear that.
BARRY. Goin' a drop 'em!
COLIN. In the park?
MIKE. At 'alf-past twelve?
PETE (laughing). The dirty ol' scrubber. (LEN and MARY
    start to cross left.)
BARRY (to COLIN). That what they taught yer at school?
    (COLIN whistles.)
LEN (amused). Put a sock in it.
BARRY. What ye got at the top a your legs? What time's
    breakfast?
MARY. That your mates?
LEN. They're juss 'avin' a laugh.
MARY. You all right with them bags?
LEN. Yeh.
COLIN. Roger the lodger 'ad a bad cough.
MIKE. 'E sneezed so 'ard.
COLIN. 'Is doorknob fell off.
BARRY. 'Is landlady said we'll soon 'ave yer well.
COLIN. So she pulled off 'er drawers.
MIKE. An' polished 'is bell!
MARY. Lot a roughs. (LEN and MARY go out left.)

PETE. Makes yer think.

COLIN. What?

PETE. Never know what yer missin'.

MIKE. True.

PETE. I knew a bloke once reckoned 'e knocked off 'is grannie.

COLIN. Yeh?

PETE. All a mistake.

COLIN. 'Ow's that?

PETE. There was a power cut at the time an' —

BARRY. —'E thought it was 'is sister.

PETE. Ain' yer clever!

MIKE. Trust the unions!

COLIN. Makes yer think, though. (BARRY blows a raspberry.)

PETE (smoking his pipe). Never know 'alf what goes on.

MIKE. That age she must be 'angin' out for it.

PETE. Stuffin' it all in before it's too late.

COLIN. Yeh. (There is a slight pause.)

PETE. Ooorrr! I'll 'ave t' fix up a little bird t'night. 'Ere, wass the time?

COLIN. Time we're back t' work. (They groan.)

MIKE (to PETE). Time yer're round the church they'll 'ave 'im down the 'ole or up the chimney or wherever 'e's goin'.

PETE. I reckon they wanna put 'im down the 'ole an' pull the chain.

SCENE FOUR

The living room. Dark.

The door opens. MARY comes in. She puts on the light. HARRY is sitting in the armchair. He is partly asleep. MARY puts sauce, salt and pepper on the table and goes out. HARRY gets up. He goes to the door and puts the light out. He goes back to the armchair. Pause.

The door opens. MARY comes in. She puts on the light. She takes knife, fork, spoon and table napkin to the table. She lays the napkin as a small table cloth. The door opens. PAM comes in. She wears a slip and carries a hair brush and cosmetics. She switches on the television set. MARY goes out. Without waiting to adjust the set PAM goes to the couch and sits. She makes up her face. The door opens. MARY comes in with a plate of food.

MARY (calls). It's on the table. (She walks toward the table. To PAM.) I told you not to walk round like that. (MARY puts the food on the table and goes out. PAM goes to the television set and adjusts it. She goes back to the couch and sits. She makes up her face.)

(MARY comes back in. She stands at the doorway.)

MARY. It's on the table! That's the second time! (She goes to the television set.) I don't know 'ow they 'ave the nerve to put it on. (She switches to another channel. She steps back to look at the picture. She steps forward to adjust it. She steps back.) Hm. (She steps forward and adjusts it again.) If yer put it in the oven it goes 'ard as nails. (She steps back and looks at the set. She goes to the couch, sits and watches television. Pause.)
PAM. More like one a them daft mirrors at a circus.
MARY. The man'll 'ave to come an' fix it. (She goes to the set and adjusts it.) You don't know 'ow to switch it on. It goes all right when I do it.

(LEN comes in.)

LEN. Smells great.
MARY. You've let it ruin.
LEN. Nah.

MARY. Cold as Christmas.

LEN. Do me. (He sits at the table and eats.)

MARY (goes to the set and re-adjusts it). I don't know. — Did yer put the light out in the scullery?

LEN. Yeh.

MARY. We need a new one. That's what's wrong with it. (She goes back to the couch and sits. She watches silently. Pause.)

PAM. Looks like one a them black an' white minstrels.

MARY. Well, you do it, an' don't sit there pokin' 'oles.

PAM. I ain' watchin'.

MARY. Sounds like it. (LEN eats. MARY watches. PAM makes up. HARRY is still. The television is fairly loud. A very long pause. Slowly a baby starts to cry. It goes on crying without a break until the end of the scene. Nothing happens until it has cried a long while. Then MARY speaks.) Can yer see?

LEN. Yeh.

MARY. Move yer seat.

LEN. I can see. (Pause.) Yer a fair ol' cook.

MARY. It's ruined. Yer get no encouragement t' try. (Pause. The baby screams with rage. After a while MARY lifts her head in the direction of the screams.) Pam-laa! (Slight pause. PAM stands and puts her cosmetics in a little bag. She goes to the television set. She turns up the volume. She goes back to the couch and sits.) There's plenty of left-overs.

LEN. Full up.

MARY. An' there's rhubarb and custard.

LEN. Oh. (Pause. The baby chokes.)

PAM. Too lazy t' get up an' fetch it.

MARY. Don't start. Let's 'ave a bit a peace for one night. (Pause.)

PAM. 'Is last servant died a over-work.

LEN. I ain' finished this, nosey.

MARY. Why don't yer shut that kid up.

PAM. I can't.

MARY. Yer don't try.

PAM. Juss cries louder when I go near it.

MARY (watching television). I ain' goin' up for yer. (Still watching television.) High time it 'ad a father. (To LEN.) There's plenty a tea in the pot.

LEN (watching television). Yeh.

MARY (watching television). That's what it needs. No wonder it cries. (Pause. To LEN.) Busy?

LEN. Murder.

MARY (watching television). Weather don't 'elp.

LEN (still watching television). Eh? (The baby whimpers piti-fully. Pause. Still watching television.) Ha! (Pause. PAM picks up her things and goes out.)

MARY. About time.

LEN. Wan'a cup?

MARY. No. There's milk in that custard. It'll only get thrown out.

LEN (stands). I'll bust. (He goes out.)

MARY (calls). On the top shelf.

LEN (offstage). What?

MARY. It's on the top shelf!

(Pause. LEN comes in. He carries a plate to the table.)

MARY. Did yer get it?

LEN. Yeh. (He sits.)

MARY. Shut that door, Len. Me 'ead's playin' me up again.

LEN. Take some a yer anadins.

MARY. I've 'ad too many t'day. Thass what makes it worse. (LEN goes to the door and shuts it. He goes to the table and eats.) Did yer put the oven out?

LEN. An' the light.

MARY. I ain' made a money, y'know. (Suddenly the baby cries much louder.) Put some sugar on it. (LEN sprinkles the sugar from a teaspoon.) People'll send the police round 'ere next.

LEN. It'll cry itself t'sleep.

(PAM comes in. She wears a dress.)

MARY. It's still cryin'.

PAM. I thought the cat was stuck up the chimney. (She sits on the couch and pulls up her stockings.) 'Ad a good look? — I'm tired a 'im watchin' me all the time.

MARY. I told yer t' get dressed in the scullery like anybody else.

PAM. I can dress where I like in me own 'ome.

LEN (to himself). Oh, no.

PAM. You say somethin'?

LEN (calmly). Yeh — shut up.

PAM. I suppose that's your idea a good manners. (Pause.) When yer leavin' us? I'm sick an' tired a arstin'.

MARY. I don't wanna 'ear all this again t'night.

PAM. 'E gets on me nerves.

LEN. I ain' leavin' that kid.

PAM. Why?

LEN. With you?

PAM. It ain' your kid.

LEN. No?

PAM. Yer'll 'ave t' take my word for it.

LEN. Yer don't even know when you're lyin'. (Pause. The baby cries.)

PAM. I don't understan' yer. Yer ain' got no self respect.

LEN. You 'ave like.

PAM. No one with any self respect would wanna stay. (LEN pours tea for himself.) Yer'll 'ave t'go sometime. Yer can't juss 'ang on till yer rot.

MARY. Pack it up! No wonder that kid cries!

PAM. Why don't you tell 'im t'go? It's your job. 'E's gettin' on me nerves every night. If it goes on much longer I'll be ill.

MARY. That'll teach yer t'bring fellas back.

PAM (to HARRY). Why don't you tell 'im? It's your 'ouse. There's bin nothin' but rows an' arguments ever since 'e got 'ere. I've 'ad all I can stand! (Slight pause.) Dad!

HARRY. I ain' gettin' involved. Bound t'be wrong.

PAM (to LEN). I don't understan' yer. Yer can't enjoy stayin' 'ere. (LEN drinks his tea.) It's bad enough bein' stuck with a kid without 'avin' you 'anging roun' me neck. The 'ole street's laughin' be'ind yer back.

LEN. I ain' leavin' that kid.

PAM. Take it.

LEN. With me?

PAM. 'Ow else?

MARY. 'Ow can 'e?

PAM. Thass 'is worry.

MARY. 'E can't look after a kid.

PAM. Put it on the council.

MARY (shrugs). They wouldn't 'ave it if they've got any sense. (The baby cries.)

PAM. Well?

LEN. Kids need proper 'omes.

PAM. Yer see!

LEN (looks in the teapot). Out a water. (He goes out.)

MARY. Wouldn't yer miss it?

PAM. That racket? (The baby whimpers. There is a ring. PAM goes out. MARY quickly tidies the couch.)

(LEN comes back with the teapot.)

MARY. Did the door go?

LEN (nods). Juss then.

FRED (offstage). All right, all right. I said I'm sorry, ain' I? (PAM is heard indistinctly.) Well, let's say 'allo first!

(FRED comes in.)

FRED. 'Evenin'. 'Evenin', ma.
MARY. We're just watchin' telly.
FRED. Anythin' interestin'?
MARY. Come in.
FRED. 'Lo, Len. 'Ow's life?
LEN. Usual. 'Ow's the job?
FRED. Don't talk about it.

(PAM comes in.)

PAM. I still don't see 'ow that makes yer all this late.
FRED. Give it a rest, Pam.
PAM. The same last time.
MARY. Take yer coat off.
PAM. Yer oughta let me know if yer're goin'a be late.
FRED. 'Ow could I? Sorry, love. We'll juss 'ave t' make it
    later in future.
PAM (to MARY). Can I put the kid in your room?
MARY. No wonder it can't sleep. Pushed around like some
    ol' door mat.
PAM. Can I or can't I? I ain' sittin' there with that row goin'
    on.
MARY. Do what yer like.
FRED (to PAM). Got plenty a fags?
MARY. Yer will anyway.
PAM (to FRED). Ready?
FRED. See yer, Lenny boy.
LEN. Yeh.
PAM. It's all the same if I was meetin' yer outside in the street.
    I'd be left standin' in the cold.
FRED (following PAM to the door). Got any fags? I left mine
    be'ind. (PAM and FRED go out. LEN stacks the things on
    the table and takes some of them out. The baby's crying
    suddenly gets louder.)

(LEN comes in again. He picks up the sauce and the table napkin
    and goes out. MARY turns off the television set and goes
    out. HARRY goes to the table and pours himself tea. LEN
    comes back.)

LEN. Oh.

HARRY. Finished.

LEN. Ta. (Pause.) Wish t'God I could take that kid out a this.

HARRY (drinks). Better.

LEN. No life growin' up 'ere.

HARRY (wipes his mouth on the back of his hand). Ah.

LEN. Wish t'God I 'ad some place.

HARRY. Yer wan'a keep yer door shut.

LEN. What?

HARRY. T'night.

LEN. Me door?

HARRY. Yer always keep your door open when 'e's sleepin'
    with 'er.

LEN. I listen out for the kid. They ain' bothered.

MARY (offstage). Night, Len.

LEN (calls). Night. (To HARRY.) More?

HARRY. No.

LEN. Plenty in the pot.

HARRY (wipes his mouth on the back of his hand). Yer'll
    catch cold with it open.

LEN (holding the teapot). Night, then. (He goes to the door.)

HARRY (sitting in the armchair). Put that light out. (LEN
    puts the light out and goes. The crying sobs away to silence.)

SCENE FIVE

Len's bedroom. It is shaped like the living room. Furniture:
    A single bed up right, a wooden chair close to it. PAM is

in bed. LEN stands center, away from her.

LEN.   Did yer take yer medicine?   (Pause.)   Feelin' better?
PAM.   I'm movin' down t' me own room t'morra. Yer'll 'ave
   t' move back up 'ere.
LEN. Quieter up 'ere.
PAM. Like a blinkin' grave.
LEN. Why don't yer 'ave the telly up?
PAM. No.
LEN. Easy fix a plug.
PAM. Did yer see Fred?
LEN.   Yer never took yer medicine.   (He pours her medicine
   and gives it to her.) 'Ere. (PAM takes it.) Say ta. (She
   drinks it and gives a small genuine "Ugh!") Read yer maga-
   zines?
PAM. Did Fred say anythin'?
MARY (offstage). Pam-laa! She gettin' up, Len?
PAM (to herself). Oh, God.
MARY (offstage). The doctor says there's nothin' t' stop yer
   gettin' up. Yer're as well as I am. (LEN closes the door but
   the voice is still heard.) Pam-laa! The dinner's on the table.
LEN. Yer better off up 'ere out a 'er way.
PAM. The cow. (LEN straightens the bed.) Leave that.
LEN. You're comin' undone.
PAM. Leave it.
LEN. It's all —
PAM. I said leave it!
LEN (continuing). Someone's got a give yer a 'and.
PAM. I won't 'ave yer pullin' me about.
LEN (walking away). Why don't yer sit in a chair for 'alf 'our?
PAM. Mind yer own business.
LEN. Yer ain't doin' yerself no good lyin' there.
MARY (offstage). She gettin' up?
LEN. I'm only tryin' a 'elp.
PAM. Don't want yer 'elp.

LEN. Yer got bugger all idea 'ow to look after yerself.

PAM. Go away.

LEN. Some one —

PAM. For Chrissake!

LEN. Someone's got a stick up for yer. (Slight pause.) Yer treated me like dirt. But I ain't goin' a carry on like that.

MARY (offstage). Pamm-laa!

PAM (calls). Shut up! I'm sick a the lot of yer! (Slight pause.) Shut up! (LEN goes out.) Thank Chriss for that.

MARY (offstage). She up yet? (LEN answers indistinctly. Pause.)

(PAM pulls out the blankets that LEN tucked in. LEN comes back with the baby.)

LEN (to baby). 'Ello then! 'Ello then!

PAM. Oh, no.

LEN. Look-ee that. 'Oo that mummy-there?

PAM. She's got the grub out on the table.

LEN. It'll keep.

PAM. She ain' better row me out for it.

LEN. Take it.

PAM. Put it back.

LEN. Yer ought a take it.

PAM. Don't keep tellin' me what I ought a do.

LEN. Yer ain' even looked at it for weeks.

PAM. Ain' going to.

LEN. Yer'd feel better. (Pause.) 'Ello then.

PAM. Did yer give 'im what I wrote?

LEN. 'E's busy, 'e reckons. It's 'is busy time.

PAM. Ha!

LEN. 'Avin' yourn on a tray?

PAM. If yer like.

LEN. It knows yer voice.

PAM. Put it away before it starts.

LEN. Good for its lungs.

PAM. Yer d'narf annoy me, Len.

LEN. I know.

PAM. Yer're always pesterin' me.

LEN. Someone's got a look after yer.

PAM. There yer are! Thass another annoyin' thing t' say. (She sits.) This dump gives me the 'ump. Put that away.

LEN. Yer can't let it lie on its back all day. Someone's got a pick it up.

PAM (sitting back). Why should I worry? Its father don't give a damn. I could be dyin' an' 'e can't find ten minutes.

LEN. I'm blowed if I'm goin' a put meself out if yer can't cooperate. (He tries to put the baby in her arms.)

PAM. I tol' yer take it back! Get off a me! Yer bloody lunatic! Bleedin' cheek! (Calls.) Mum!

LEN. You 'ave it for a change! (He puts the baby on the bed.)

PAM. Yer goin' mad! It's fallin'. Catch it! (LEN puts the baby so that it is safe.)

LEN. I ain' your paid nurse!

PAM (calls). Mum! — I know why Fred ain' come — yer bin tearin' up me letters.

LEN. 'E did!

PAM. Yer little liar! (She turns away from the baby.) I ain' touchin' it.

LEN. It'll stay there all night!

PAM. Thass what yer call 'elpin' me. (Pause. LEN picks up the baby.) See!

LEN. Can't give it a cold juss because we're rowin'. (He goes toward the door. He stops.) 'E said 'e'd look in.

PAM (turns around). When? (She turns back to the wall.) What did 'e say?

LEN. I said yer wanted to see 'im. 'E goes 'e's up to 'is eyes in it. So I said I got a couple of tickets for Crystal Palace. 'E's knockin' off early.

PAM. Saturday?

LEN. T'night.

PAM (turns). Yer got 'im downstairs!

LEN. No.

PAM (calls). Mum — is Fred there? Fred? — 'E might be early.

LEN. There's a good 'alf 'our yet.

PAM (excited). I 'ope 'is lot wins.

LEN. 'E might be late.

PAM. Not for football. Yer can say she's uptairs if yer wan'a
    go. Put it like that.

LEN (looks at child). 'E's well away.

PAM. I ain' cut me nails all the time I bin in bed.

MARY (offstage). Lennie!

LEN. Shall I get the scissors?

PAM. She won't shut up till yer go down. I got me own.

MARY (offstage). Leonard! I keep callin' yer. (Outside the
    door.) 'Ow many more times.

(MARY comes in.)

MARY. I bin callin' the last 'alf 'our. Dinner won't be fit t'eat.

LEN. Juss puttin' the nipper back.

MARY. That's the last time I cook a 'ot meal in this 'ouse.
    I mean it this time. (To PAM.) Yer can make yer own bed
    t'morra, you. (To LEN.) I ain' sweatin' over a 'ot stove.
    No one offers t'buy me a new one. (To PAM.) I can't afford
    t' keep yer on yer national 'ealth no longer. I'm the one
    'oo ought to be in bed. (She goes out.)

PAM. I got all patches under me eyes.

LEN. No.

PAM. I feel awful.

LEN. Yer look nice.

PAM. I'll 'ave t' 'ave a wash.

LEN. Yeh.

SCENE SIX

The park. A bare stage. FRED holds a fishing rod out over the
    stalls. He wears jeans and an old dull leather jacket. LEN
    sits beside him on a small tin box. On the ground there is
    a bait box, odds and ends box, float box, milk bottle, sugar
    bottle, flask and net.

LEN. Round our place t'night?
FRED. No.
LEN. It's Saturday.
FRED. Oh, yeh.
LEN. She won't like it.
FRED. No. (Pause.) Yer wan'a get yerself a good rod.
LEN. Can't afford it.
FRED. Suit yerself.
LEN. Lend us yourn.
FRED. Get knotted. (Slight pause.)
LEN. I in yer way then?
FRED. Eh?
LEN. Sittin' 'ere.
FRED. Free country.
LEN. Yer'd never think it.
FRED. Nippy.
LEN. Lend us yer jacket.
FRED. Jump in.
LEN. 'Ow much yer give for that?
FRED. Yer get 'em on h.p.
LEN. Fair bit a work.
FRED (runs his hand along the rod). Comes in 'andy. (Pause.)
LEN. She said yer was comin' round for the telly.
FRED. News t' me.
LEN. Don't know whass on.

FRED. Don't care.

LEN. Never looked. (Slight pause.) Never bothers me. Easy find out from the paper if yer —

FRED. Don't keep on about it.

LEN. Eh?

FRED. Don't bloody well keep on about it.

LEN. Suits me. (Slight pause.) I was agreein' with yer. I thought like —

FRED. Oi — Len, I come out for the fishin'. I don't wanna 'ear all your ol' crap. (Slight pause. LEN turns his head right and stares at the river.) 'Onest, Len — yer d'narf go on.

LEN. I only said I was agreein' with yer. Blimey, if yer can't . . . (He stops. Pause.)

FRED. Sod!

LEN. Whass up?

FRED. Bait's gone.

LEN. Gone? They've 'ad it away.

FRED. Never.

LEN. Must 'ave.

FRED. More like wriggled off.

LEN. I mounted it 'ow yer said.

FRED (winds in). Come 'ere. Look. (He takes a worm from the worm box.) Right. Yer take yer worm. Yer roll it in yer 'and t' knock it out. Thass first. Then yer break a bit off. Cop 'old o' that. (He gives part of the worm to LEN.)

LEN. Ta.

FRED. Now yer thread yer 'ook through this bit. Push it up on yer gut. Leave it. — Give us that bit. Ta. Yer thread yer other bit on the 'ook, but her leave a fair bit 'angin' off like that, why, t'wriggle in the water. Then yer push yer top bit down off the gut and camer-flarge yer shank. Got it?

LEN. Thass 'ow I done it.

FRED. Yeh. Main thing, keep it neat. (He casts. The line hums.) Lovely. (A long silence.) The life. (Silence.)

LEN. Down the labor Monday. (FRED grunts.) Start somethin'.

(Silence.) No life, broke.

FRED. True. (Silence. LEN pokes in the worm box with a stick.) Feed 'em on milk.

LEN. Fact? (Silence.) I'll tell 'er yer ain' comin'.

FRED. Len!

LEN. Well, yer got a let 'er know.

FRED. 'Oo says?

LEN. Yer can't juss —

FRED. Well?

LEN. Shut up a minute.

FRED. Listen, mate, shut yer trap an' give us a snout.

LEN. No.

FRED. Yer're loaded.

LEN. Scroungin' git! Smoke yer own. — She'll be up 'alf the night. That'll be great. — I reckon yer got a bloody nerve takin' my fags, yer know I'm broke. — Yer believe in keepin' 'em waitin' for it. (Slight pause.)

FRED. Yer used to knock 'er off, that right?

LEN. Once.

FRED. There yer are then.

LEN. What?

FRED. It's all yourn.

LEN. She don't wan'a now.

FRED. 'Ow's that?

LEN. Since you 'ad 'er.

FRED. What d'yer expect? No — they're like that. Once they go off, they go right off.

LEN. Don't even get a feel.

FRED. 'Appens all the time. Give us a snout.

LEN. No.

FRED. Tight arse. (Slight pause.)

LEN. Skip?

FRED. Yeh?

LEN. What yer reckon on 'er?

FRED. For a lay?

LEN. Yeh.

FRED. Fair. Depends on the bloke.

LEN. Well?

FRED. No – get that any time. (Silence.)

LEN. Gettin' dark. (Silence.)

FRED. Call it a day.

LEN. In a minute.

FRED. Never know why yer stick that dump.

LEN. Seen worse.

FRED. I ain'. (Slight pause.)

LEN. Skip?

FRED. Whass up now?

LEN. Why's she go for you?

FRED. They all do, mate.

LEN. No, why's she – ill over it?

FRED. Come off it, she 'ad a drop a the ol' flu.

LEN. Yeh. But why's she like that?

FRED. It ain' me money.

LEN. They all want the same thing, I reckon. So you must 'ave more a it.

FRED. Thass true! Oi!

LEN. What?

FRED. Still. (Pause.) Thought I 'ad a touch. (Pause.) Nah. (They ease off. FRED looks up at the sky.) Jack it in.

LEN. Anyway, thass what they reckon.

FRED. Eh?

LEN. They all want the same thing.

FRED. Oh.

LEN. I reckon yer're 'avin' me on.

FRED. Me?

LEN. Like the fish that got away.

FRED. I ain' with yer. (He shakes his head.)

LEN. That big! (He holds his hands eighteen inches apart.)

FRED (laughs). More like that! (He holds his hands three feet apart.)

LEN. Ha! Thass why she's sick.

FRED. Now give us a fag.

LEN. No.

FRED (spits). 'Ave t' light one a me own. (He takes one of his own cigarettes from a packet in his breast pocket. He does not take the packet from the pocket.)

LEN. Mind the moths.

FRED. Yer ever 'ad worms up yer nose, in yer ears, an' down yer throat?

LEN. Not lately.

FRED. Yer will in a minute.

LEN. Well, give us a snout then.

FRED. Slimey ponce! (He gives LEN a cigarette. LEN gives FRED a light.)

LEN. I used a 'ear, know that?

FRED. 'Ear what? — 'E's like a flippin' riddle.

LEN. You an' 'er.

FRED. Me an' 'oo?

LEN. On the bash.

FRED. Do what?

LEN. Straight up.

FRED. Chriss.

LEN. Yeh.

FRED. Yer kiddin'.

LEN. On my life. Kep me up 'alf the night. Yer must a bin trying for the cup.

FRED (draws his cigarette). Why didn't yer let on?

LEN. No, it's all a giggle, ain't it?

FRED (shrugs). Yeh? Makes yer feel a right charlie. (He drops his cigarette on the floor and treads on it.) Chriss. Thass one good reason for jackin' 'er in.

LEN. Don't start blamin' me.

FRED. An' you was listenin'?

LEN. Couldn't 'elp it.

FRED. Oh. (He lays his rod on the ground and crouches to pack his things.) Yer didn't mind me goin' round 'er's.

LEN. Same if I did.

FRED. I didn't know like.

LEN. Yer never ruddy thought. Any'ow, I don't mind.

FRED. I thought she was goin' spare.

LEN. Wan'a 'and?

FRED. No. Give us that tin. (He packs in silence.) I reckon it was up t' you t' say. Yer got a tongue in yer 'ead. (Silence.)

(MIKE comes in. He has a haversack slung from one shoulder and carries a rod. He wears a small, flashy hat.)

FRED. No luck?

MIKE. Wouldn't feed a cat.

LEN. Waste a time.

MIKE. Same 'ere.

FRED. Got a breeze up.

MIKE. What yer doin'?

FRED. Now?

MIKE. Yeh, t'night.

FRED. Reckon anythin'?

MIKE. Bit a fun.

FRED. Suits me .

MIKE. You're on.

FRED. Up the other end?

MIKE. 'Ow's the cash?

FRED. Broke. You?

MIKE. I'll touch up the ol' lady.

FRED. Get a couple for me.

LEN. That'll pay the fares.

MIKE. Pick yer up roun' your place.

FRED. Not too early. 'Ave a bath first.

MIKE. Never know 'oo yer'll be sleepin' with.

FRED. After eight.

MIKE. I feel juss right for it.

LEN. What?

MIKE. Out on the 'unt.

FRED (imitates a bullet). Tschewwwww!

MIKE. 'E picks 'em up at a 'undred yards.

FRED. It's me magnetic cobblers.

(PAM comes in. She pushes the pram. The hood is up. A long blue sausage balloon floats from a corner of the hood.)

PAM. 'Ello.

FRED. Whass up?

PAM. Out for a walk.

MIKE (nods at pram). Bit late for that, ain't it?

PAM (to FRED). What yer got?

FRED. Nothin'.

PAM (tries to look). Less 'ave a look.

FRED. Nothin' for you!

PAM. Keep yer shirt on.

MIKE. Yer nearly missed us.

PAM (to FRED). Don't get so 'airy-ated.

MIKE. We was juss off.

FRED. What yer cartin' that about for?

PAM. Felt like a walk.

FRED. Bit late.

PAM. Why?

FRED. That ought a be in bed.

PAM. Fresh air won't kill it.

FRED. Should a done it earlier.

PAM. Never 'ad time. Why didn't you?

FRED. You know best.

PAM. When yer comin' round?

FRED. I'll look in.

PAM. When?

FRED. I don't know.

PAM. When about?

FRED. Later on.

PAM. Shall I get somethin' to eat?

FRED. No.

PAM. No bother.

FRED. The ol' lady'll 'ave it all set up.

PAM. I got two nice chops.

FRED. Shame.

PAM. Well, see 'ow yer feel. There's no one in now. I got rid a 'em.

FRED. Pity yer didn't say.

PAM. What time then?

FRED. I'll be there.

PAM. Sure?

FRED. Yeh.

PAM. Say so if yer ain'.

FRED. I'll be there.

PAM. That means yer won't.

FRED. Up t'you.

PAM. Why don't yer say so?

FRED (picks up gear; to MIKE). Thass the lot.

PAM. It ain' no fun waitin' in all night for nothin'.

MIKE. Ready?

FRED (takes a look around). Yeh.

PAM. Why can't yer tell the truth for once?

FRED. Fair enough. I ain' comin'.

LEN. Pam —

PAM. Yer 'ad no intention a comin'.

LEN. Yer left the brake off again.

MIKE (to FRED). Okay?

PAM (to LEN). Put it on, clever.

FRED (to MIKE). Yeh.

PAM (to FRED). I knew all along.

FRED. Come on, Pam. Go 'ome.

PAM. Fred.

FRED. I know.

PAM. I didn't mean t' go off. I was goin' a be nice, I still ain'
    better.

FRED. Go 'ome an' get in the warm. It's late.

LEN (putting on the brake). Yer wan'a be more carefui.

PAM (to FRED). It's my fault. I never stop t'think.

FRED. Yer wan'a stop thinkin' about yerself, I know that.

PAM. It's them pills they give me.

MIKE (to FRED). You comin' or ain' yer.

FRED. Yeh.

PAM. No.

FRED. I'll come round one night next week.

PAM. No.

FRED. Monday night. 'Ow's that?

PAM. Yer'll change yer mind.

FRED. Straight from work.

PAM. Yer said that before.

FRED. It's the best I can offer.

PAM. I can't go back there now.

FRED. Yer'll be okay.

PAM. If I sit on me own in that room another night I'll go
    round the bend.

FRED. Yer got the kid.

PAM. Juss t'night. I couldn't stand it on me own no more. I
    'ad a come out. I don't know what I'm doin'. That kid ought
    a be in bed. Less take it 'ome, Fred. It's 'ad new-moanier
    once.

FRED. You take it 'ome.

PAM. Juss this last time? I won't arst no more. I'll get mum
    t' stay in with me.

FRED. It's no use.

PAM. Yer ain' seen it in a long time, 'ave yer? (She turns the
    pram around.) It's puttin' on weight.

FRED. Eh?

PAM. It don't cry like it used to. Not all the time.

MIKE. Past carin'.

PAM. Doo-dee-doo-dee. Say da-daa.

FRED. Yeh, lovely. (He looks away.)

LEN (looking at the baby). Blind.

PAM (to LEN). Like a top.

FRED. What yer give it?

PAM. Asprins.

FRED. That all right?

PAM. Won't wake up till t'morra. It won't disturb yer. What time'll I see yer?

FRED. I'll look in. I ain' sayin' definite.

PAM. I don't mind. Long as I know yer're comin'.

FRED. All right.

PAM. Pity t' waste the chops. I think I'll do 'em in case —

FRED. Yeh, right. It's all accordin'.

PAM. I'll wait up.

FRED. It'll be late, see.

PAM. Thass all right.

FRED. Pam.

PAM. I'll treat meself t' box a choclits.

FRED. There's plenty a blokes knockin' about. Why don't yer pick on someone else.

PAM. No.

MIKE. Yer can 'ave me, darlin'. But yer'll 'ave t' learn a bit more respect.

PAM. 'Ow can I get out with that 'angin' round me neck? 'Oo's goin' a look at me?

FRED. Yer ol' girl'll take it off yer 'ands.

MIKE. Drop 'er a few bob.

FRED. Yer don't try.

PAM. I can't!

FRED. Yer'll 'ave to.

PAM. I can't! I ain' goin' to!

FRED. I ain' goin' a see yer no more.

PAM. No.

FRED. We got a sort this out some time.

PAM. Yer promised!

FRED. It's a waste a time!

PAM. They 'eard!

FRED. No.

MIKE. Come on, mate.

FRED. It's finished.

MIKE. Thank Chriss. Less shift!

PAM. Juss t'night. I don't care if yer bin with yer girls. Come 'ome after. Juss once. I won't bother yer. I'll let yer sleep. Please.

FRED. Chriss.

PAM. Oh, what d'you care? I was flat on me back three bloody weeks! 'Oo lifted a finger? I could a bin dyin'! No one! (She starts pushing the pram.)

MIKE. Good riddance!

PAM (stops). You're that kid's father! Yeh! Yer ain't wrigglin' out a that!

FRED. Prove it.

PAM. I *know*!

FRED. You *know*?

MIKE. Chriss.

FRED. 'Alf the bloody manor's bin through you.

PAM. Rotten liar!

FRED. Yeh? (To MIKE.) Ain' you 'ad 'er?

MIKE. Not yet.

FRED. Yer'll be next. (Points to LEN.) What about 'im? (To LEN.) Eh? (To MIKE.) Your's must be the only stiff outside the churchyard she ain' knocked off.

PAM. I 'ate you!

FRED. Now we're gettin' somewhere.

PAM. Pig!

FRED. Thass better. Now piss off!

PAM. I will.

MIKE. Ta-ta!

PAM. An' yer can take yer bloody bastard round yer tart's! Tell 'er it's a present from me! (PAM goes out. She leaves the pram.)

MIKE. Lovely start t' the evenin's entertainment.

FRED (calls). I ain' takin' it! It'll bloody stay 'ere!

MIKE. What yer wan'a let 'er get away with —

FRED. Don't you start! I 'ad enough with 'er!

LEN. I'd better go after 'er.

FRED. Send 'er back.

LEN. See 'ow she is. (LEN goes out after Pam.)

FRED (calls). Don't leave 'er kid. Take it with yer. (MIKE whistles after Pam. FRED throws his gear down.) Lumbered!

MIKE. 'E'll send 'er back.

FRED. 'E ain' got the gumption. We'll drop it in on the way back.

MIKE. Leave it 'ere. Won't be worth goin' time we're ready.

FRED. Give it five minutes.

MIKE. Yer won't see 'er again.

FRED. That won't be the worst thing in me life.

MIKE. Can't yer arst your Liz t' look after it?

FRED. She'd tear me eyes out. (Pause. They sit.)

MIKE. They opened that new church on the corner.

FRED. What?

MIKE. They got a club.

FRED. Oh, yeh.

MIKE. We'll 'ave a quick little case round.

FRED. T'night?

MIKE. Yeh.

FRED. Get stuffed.

MIKE. Straight up.

FRED. Pull the other one.

MIKE. Best place out for'n easy pick up.

FRED. Since when?

MIKE. I done it before. There's little pieces all over the shop, nothin' a do.

FRED. Fact?

MIKE. The ol' bleeder shuts 'is eyes for prayers an' they're touchin' 'em all over the place. Then the law raided this one an' they 'ad it shut down.

FRED. Do leave off.

(PETE and COLIN come in right.)

PETE. 'Ow's it then?

MIKE. Buggered up.

COLIN. Like your arse.

MIKE. Like your flippin' ear in a minute.

PETE. I – I!

COLIN. Wass on t'night?

MIKE. Laugh.

(BARRY comes in after Pete and Colin.)

BARRY. Fishin'?

FRED. 'Angin' the Chrissmas decorations.

BARRY. 'Oo's bin chuckin' big dog ends?

MIKE. Where?

BARRY. 'Ardly bin lit.

PETE. 'E's juss waitin' for us t'shift an' 'e'll be on it.

FRED (holds it out). On the 'ouse.

MIKE. 'As 'e got a little tin?

COLIN. Like 'n ol' tramp?

BARRY. Oh, yeh – 'oo's mindin' the baby?

COLIN (seeing pram). Wass that for?

MIKE. Pushin' the spuds in.

FRED (flicks the dog end to BARRY). Catch!

COLIN. 'Oo left it 'ere?

BARRY. 'E's takin' it for a walk.

PETE. Nice.

FRED. Piss off.

BARRY. We don't wan' the little nipper t'ear that! Oi, come

'ere. (COLIN and PETE go to the pram.) Oo's 'e look like? (They laugh.)

MIKE. Don't stick your ugly mug in its face!

PETE. It'll crap itself t' death.

BARRY. Dad'll change its nappies.

COLIN (amused). Bloody nutter!

FRED. You wake it up an' yer can put it t'sleep. (COLIN and PETE laugh.)

BARRY. Put it t'sleep?

COLIN. 'E'll put it t'sleep for good.

PETE. With a brick.

MIKE. 'E don't care if it's awake all night.

BARRY. 'Oo don't? I'm like a bloody uncle t' the kids round our way. (He pushes the pram.) Doo-dee-doo-dee-doo-dee.

MIKE (to FRED). Jack it in, eh?

FRED. Give 'er another minute.

MIKE. We should a made Len stay with it.

FRED. Slipped up. 'E dodged off bloody sharpish.

MIKE. Sly bleeder.

FRED. I don't know — bloody women!

MIKE. Know a better way? (FRED and MIKE are sititng down left. PETE and COLIN are right. BARRY pushes the pram.)

BARRY.

> Rock a bye baby on a tree top
> When the wind blows the cradle will rock
> When the bough breaks the cradle will fall
> And down will come baby and cradle and tree
>> an' bash its little brains out an' dad'll scoop
>> 'em up and use 'em for bait

(They laugh.)

FRED. Save money. (BARRY takes the balloon. He poses with it.)

COLIN. Thought they was pink now.

BARRY (pokes at Colin's head). Come t' the pictures t'night, darlin'? (He bends it.) It's got a bend in it.

MIKE. Don't take after its dad.

BARRY (blows it up). 'Ow's that then?

COLIN. Go easy.

BARRY (blows again). Thass more like it. (Blows again.)

COLIN. Do leave off.

MIKE. That reminds me, I said I'd meet the girl t'night. (BARRY blows. The balloon bursts.)

COLIN. Got me! (He falls dead. BARRY pushes the pram over him.) Get off! I'll 'ave a new suit out a you.

BARRY (pushing the pram around). Off the same barrer?

PETE. Ain' seen you 'ere before, darlin'.

BARRY. 'Op it!

PETE. 'Ow about poppin' in the bushes?

COLIN. Two's up.

BARRY. What about the nipper?

PETE. Too young for me. (He "touches" BARRY.)

BARRY. 'Ere! Dirty bastard! (He projects the pram viciously after COLIN. It hits PETE.)

PETE. Bastard! (PETE and BARRY look at each other. PETE gets ready to push the pram back — but plays at keeping BARRY guessing. MIKE and FRED are heard talking in their corner.)

MIKE. If there's nothin' in the church, know what?

FRED. No.

MIKE. Do the all-night laundries.

FRED. Yer got a 'and it to yer for tryin'.

MIKE. Yer get all them little 'ousewives there.

FRED. Bit past it though.

MIKE. Yeh, but all right. (PETE pushes the pram violently at BARRY. He catches it straight on the flat of his boot and sends it back with the utmost ferocity. PETE sidesteps. COLIN stops it.)

PETE. Stupid git!

COLIN. Wass up with 'im?

BARRY. Keep yer dirty 'ands off me!

PETE. 'E'll 'ave the little perisher out!

BARRY. Oh, yeh? An' 'oo reckoned they run a kid down?

PETE. Thass different.

BARRY. Yeh – no one t' see yer. (PETE pulls the pram from COLIN, spins it around and pushes it violently at BARRY. BARRY sidesteps and catches it by the handle as it goes past.) Oi – oi! (He looks in the pram.)

COLIN. Wass up? (COLIN and PETE come over.) It can't open its eyes.

BARRY. Yer woke it.

PETE. Look at its fists.

COLIN. Yeh.

PETE. It's tryin' a clout 'im.

COLIN. Don't blame it.

PETE. Goin' a be a boxer.

BARRY. Is it a girl?

PETE. Yer wouldn't know the difference.

BARRY. 'Ow d'yer get 'em t'sleep?

PETE. Pull their 'air.

COLIN. Eh?

PETE. Like that. (He pulls its hair.)

COLIN. That 'urt. (They laugh.)

MIKE. Wass 'e doin'?

COLIN. Pullin' its 'air.

FRED. 'E'll 'ave its ol' woman after 'im.

MIKE. Poor sod.

BARRY. 'E's showin' off.

COLIN. 'E wants the coroner's medal.

MIKE (comes to the pram). Less see yer do it. (PETE pulls its hair.) Oh, yeh.

BARRY. It don't say nothin'.

COLIN. Little bleeder's 'alf dead a fright.

MIKE. Still awake.

PETE. Ain' co-operatin'.

BARRY. Try a pinch.

MIKE. That ought a work.

BARRY. Like this. (He pinches the baby.)

COLIN. Look at that mouth.

BARRY. Flippin' yawn.

PETE. Least it's tryin'.

MIKE. Pull its drawers off.

COLIN. Yeh!

MIKE. Less case its ol' crutch.

PETE. Ha!

BARRY. Yeh! (He throws the nappy in the air.) Yippee!

COLIN. Look at that! (They laugh.)

MIKE. Look at its little legs goin'.

COLIN. Ain' they ugly!

BARRY. Ugh!

MIKE. Can't keep 'em still!

PETE. 'Avin' a fit.

BARRY. It's dirty. (They groan.)

COLIN. 'Old its nose.

MIKE. Thass for 'iccups.

BARRY. Gob its crutch. (He spits.)

MIKE. Yeh!

COLIN. Ha! (He spits.)

MIKE. Got it!

PETE. Give it a punch.

MIKE. Yeh, less!

COLIN. There's no one about! (PETE punches it.) Ugh! Mind
    yer don't 'urt it.

MIKE. Yer can't.

BARRY. Not at that age.

MIKE. Course yer can't, no feelin's.

PETE. Like animals.

MIKE. 'It it again.

COLIN. I can't see!

BARRY. 'Arder.

PETE. Yeh.

BARRY. Like that! (He hits it.)

COLIN. An' that! (He also hits it.)

MIKE. What a giggle!

PETE. Cloutin's good for 'em. I read it.

BARRY (to FRED). Why don't you clout it?

FRED. It ain' mine.

PETE. Sherker. Yer got a do yer duty.

FRED. Ain' my worry. Serves 'er right.

BARRY. 'Ere, can I piss on it?

COLIN. Gungy bastard!

MIKE. Got any matches? (They laugh.)

PETE. Couldn't yer break them little fingers easy though?

COLIN. Snap!

PETE. Know what they used a do?

MIKE. Yeh.

PETE. Smother 'em.

BARRY. Yeh. That'd be somethin'.

COLIN. Looks like a yeller-nigger.

BARRY. 'Onk like a yid.

FRED. Leave it alone.

PETE. Why?

FRED. Yer don't wan' a row.

PETE. What row?

MIKE. What kid?

COLIN. I ain' seen no kid.

BARRY. Not me!

PETE. Yer wouldn't grass on yer muckers?

FRED. Grow up.

BARRY. D'narf look ill. Stupid bastard. (He jerks the pram violently.)

PETE. Thass 'ow they 'ang yer — give yer a jerk.

MIKE. Reckon it'll grow up an idiot.

PETE. Or deformed.

BARRY. Look where it come from.

PETE. Little bleeder. (He jerks the pram violently.) That

knocked the grin off its face.

MIKE. Look! Ugh!

BARRY. Look!

COLIN. What? (They all groan.)

PETE. Rub the little bastard's face in it!

BARRY. Yeh!

PETE. Less 'ave it! (He rubs the baby. They all groan.)

BARRY. Less 'ave a go! I always wan'ed a do that!

PETE. Ain' yer done it before? (BARRY does it. He laughs.)

COLIN. It's all in its eyes. (Silence.)

FRED. There'll be a row.

MIKE. It can't talk.

PETE. 'Oo cares?

FRED. I tol' yer.

COLIN. Shut up.

BARRY. I noticed 'e ain' touched it.

COLIN. Too bloody windy.

FRED. Yeh?

PETE. Less see yer.

BARRY. Yeh.

PETE. 'Fraid she'll ruck yer.

FRED. Ha! (He looks in the pram.) Chriss.

PETE. Less see yer chuck that. (PETE throws a stone to FRED. FRED doesn't try to catch it. It falls on the ground. COLIN picks it up and gives it to FRED.)

MIKE (quietly). Reckon it's all right?

COLIN (quietly). No one around.

PETE (quietly). They don't know it's us.

MIKE (quietly). She left it.

BARRY. It's done now.

PETE (quietly). Yer can do what yer like.

BARRY. Might as well enjoy ourselves.

PETE (quietly). Yer don't get a chance like this every day. (FRED throws the stone.)

COLIN. Missed.

PETE. That ain't! (He throws a stone.)

BARRY. Or that! (He throws a stone.)

MIKE. Yeh!

COLIN (running around). Where's all the stones?

MIKE (also running around). Stick it up the fair!

PETE. Liven 'Ampstead 'eath! Three throws a quid! Make a packet.

MIKE (throws a stone). Ouch!

COLIN. 'Ear that?

BARRY. Give us some. (He takes stones from COLIN.)

COLIN (throws a stone). Right in the lug 'ole. (FRED looks for a stone.)

PETE. Get its 'ooter.

BARRY. An' its slasher!

FRED (picks up a stone, spits on it). For luck, the sod. (He throws.)

BARRY. Yyooowwww!

MIKE. 'Ear it plonk! (A bell rings.)

MIKE. 'Oo's got the matches? (He finds some in his pocket.)

BARRY. What ye doin'?

COLIN. Wan'a buck up!

MIKE. Keep a look out. (He starts to throw burning matches in the pram. BARRY throws a stone. It just misses MIKE.) Look out, yer bleedin' git!

COLIN. Guy Fawkes!

PETE. Bloody nutter! Put that out!

MIKE. No! You 'ad what you want!

PETE. Yer'll 'ave the ol' bloody park 'ere! (A bell rings.)

BARRY. Piss on it! Piss on it!

COLIN. Gungy slasher.

MIKE. Call the R.S.P.C.A. (A bell rings.)

FRED. They'll shut the gates.

PETE (going). There's an 'ole in the railin's.

BARRY. 'Old on. (He looks for a stone.)

PETE. Leave it!

BARRY. Juss this one! (He throws a stone as PETE pushes him over. It goes wide.) Bastard! (To PETE.) Yer put me off!

PETE. I'll throttle yer!

BARRY. I got a get it once more! (The others have gone up left. BARRY takes a stone from the pram and throws it at point blank range. Hits.) Yar!

COLIN. Where's this 'ole!

MIKE. Yer bleedin' gear!

FRED. Chriss. (He runs down to the rod and boxes. He picks them up.)

BARRY. Bleedin' little sod! (He hacks into the pram. He goes up left.)

PETE. Come on! (A bell rings. FRED has difficulty with the boxes and rod. He throws a box away.)

FRED. 'Ang on! (He goes up left. They go off up left, making a curious buzzing. A long pause.)

(PAM comes in down left.)

PAM. I might a know'd they'd a left yer. Lucky yer got someone t' look after yer. Muggin's 'ere. (She starts to push the pram. She does not look into it. She speaks in a sing-song voice, loudly but to herself.) 'Oo's 'ad yer balloon. Thass a present from grannie. Goin' a keep me up 'alf the night? Go t' sleepies. Soon be 'ome. Nice an' warm, then. No one else wants yer. Nice an' warm. Soon be 'omies.

SCENE SEVEN

A cell. Left center a box to sit on. Otherwise, the stage is bare. A steel door bangs. FRED comes in from the left. He has a mack over his head. He sits on the case. After a slight pause he takes off the mack. Silence. A steel door bangs. PAM comes in left.

PAM. What 'appened?

FRED. Didn't yer see 'em?

PAM. I 'eard.

FRED. Bloody 'eathens. Thumpin' and kickin' the van.

PAM. 'Oo?

FRED. Bloody 'ousewives! 'Oo else? Ought a be stood up an' shot!

PAM. You all right?

FRED. No. I tol' this copper don't open the door. He goes we're 'ere, the thick bastard, an' lets 'em in. Kickin' an' punchin'. (He holds up the mack.) Look at it! Gob all over. (He throws it away from him.) 'Course I ain' all right! (Mimicking her.) "Are yer all right?"

PAM. They said I shouldn't be 'ere. But 'e was ever so nice. Said five minutes wouldn't matter.

FRED. Right bloody mess.

PAM. They can't get in 'ere.

FRED. I can't get out there!

PAM. I ain't blamin' yer.

FRED. Blamin' me? Yer got bugger all t'blame me for, mate! Yer ruined my life, thass all!

PAM. I never meant —

FRED. Why the bloody 'ell bring the little perisher out that time a night?

PAM (fingers at her mouth). I wanted a —

FRED. Yer got no right chasin' after me with a pram! Drop me right in it!

PAM. I was scared t' stay —

FRED. Never know why yer 'ad the little bleeder in the first place! Yer don't know what yer doin'! Yer're a bloody menace!

PAM. Wass it like?

FRED. They wan'a put you in, then yer'll find out. Bring any burn?

PAM. No.

FRED. Yer don't think a nothin'! Ain' yer got juss one?

PAM. No.

FRED. Yer're bloody useless.

PAM. What'll 'appen!

FRED. 'Ow do I know? I'll be the last one a know. The 'ole thing was an accident. Lot a roughs. Never seen 'em before. Don't arst me. Blokes like that anywhere. I tried to chase 'em off.

PAM. Will they believe that?

FRED. No. If I was ten years older I'd get a medal. With a crowd like our'n they got a knock someone. (He goes right.) Right bloody mess.

PAM. Yer never bin in trouble before. Juss one or two woundin's an' that.

FRED. 'Alf murdered with a lot a 'and bags!

PAM. Yer wan'a arst t' see the doctor.

FRED. Doctor! They shouldn't let him touch a sick rat with a barge pole. (He walks a few steps.) It's supposed a be grub. A starvin' cat'd walk away. (He walks a few more steps.) Wass bin 'appening?

PAM. Don't know.

FRED. On yer own?

PAM. What about them others?

FRED. What about 'em?

PAM. I could say I saw 'em.

FRED. That'd make it worse. Don't worry. I'm thinkin' it all out. This way they don't know what 'appened. Not definite. Why couldn't I bin tryin' a 'elp the kid? I got no cause t' 'arm it. (He sits on the box.)

PAM. I tol' 'em. (FRED puts his arms around Pam's waist and leans his head against her.)

FRED. Yer'll 'ave t' send us letters.

PAM. I'm buyin' a pad on me way 'ome.

FRED. Pam. I don't know what'll 'appen. There's bloody gangs like that roamin' everywhere. The bloody police don't do their job.

PAM. I'll kill meself if they touch yer.

(A steel door bangs. LEN comes in left.)

PAM. I tol' yer t' wait outside.

LEN. I got 'im some fags. (To FRED.) I 'ad a drop 'em 'alf.

PAM. 'E still won't leave me alone, Fred.

LEN. I only got a minute. They're arstin' for a remand.

FRED. Chriss. That bloody mob still outside?

LEN. They've 'emmed 'em off over the road.

FRED. Bit bloody late.

PAM. Tell 'im t' go.

LEN. We both got a go. That inspector wants you.

FRED. Where's the snout?

LEN. Put it in yer pocket.

FRED (to PAM). See yer after. (She puts her arms around him
    before he can take the cigarettes.)

PAM. I'll wait for yer.

FRED (pats her back). Yeh, yeh. God 'elp us.

LEN (to PAM). Yer'll get 'im into trouble if yer don't go.
    (FRED nods at PAM. She goes out crying.)

FRED. 'Ow many yer got?

LEN. Sixty. I 'ad a drop 'em 'alf.

FRED. Will it be all right?

LEN. Give 'em a few like, an' don't flash 'em around.

FRED. She never 'ad none. I'll do the same for you sometime.

LEN. Put 'em in yer pocket.

FRED. I don't know what I'll get.

LEN. Manslaughter. (Shrugs.) Anythin'.

FRED. It was only a kid.

LEN. I saw.

FRED. What?

LEN. I come back when I couldn't find 'er.

FRED. Yer ain't grassed?

LEN. No.
FRED. Oh.
LEN. I was in the trees. I saw the pram.
FRED. Yeh.
LEN. I saw the lot.
FRED. Yeh.
LEN. I didn't know what t'do. Well, I should a stopped yer.
FRED. Too late now.
LEN. I juss saw.
FRED. Yer saw! Yer saw! Wass the good a that? That don't
    'elp me. I'll be out in that bloody dock in a minute!
LEN. Nothin'. They got the pram in court.
FRED. Okay, okay. Reckon there's time for a quick burn?
LEN. About. (He gives FRED a light.)

INTERVAL

SCENE EIGHT

The living room. HARRY irons, LEN sits.

LEN. Yer make a fair ol' job a that. (Pause.) Don't yer get
    choked off.
HARRY. What?
LEN. That every Friday night.
HARRY. Got a keep clean.
LEN. Suppose so. (Pause.) Yer get used t' it.
HARRY. Trained to it in the army.
LEN. Oh.
HARRY. Makes a man a yer.

(MARY comes in. She looks around.)

MARY (to LEN). I wish yer wouldn't sit around in yer ol' work
    clothes an' shoes. Yer got some nice slippers. (She goes out.)
LEN. She won't let Pam.
HARRY. Eh?
LEN. She won't let Pam do that for yer.
HARRY. Don't take me long. (Long pause.)
LEN. Yer could stop 'er money. (Slight pause.) Then she
    couldn't interfere.
HARRY. Don't take long. Once yer get started.
LEN. Why don't yer try that?
HARRY. That Pam can't iron. She'd ruin 'em.
LEN. Ever thought a movin' on?
HARRY. This stuff gets dry easy.
LEN. Yer ought a think about it.
HARRY. Yer don't know what yer talking about, lad.
LEN. No. I don't.
HARRY. It's like everthin' else.
LEN. 'Ow long yer bin 'ere?
HARRY. Don't know. (He stretches his back. He irons again.)
    Yer mate's comin' out.
LEN. Yeh. Why?
HARRY. Pam's mate. (He spits on the iron.) None a it ain'
    simple.
LEN. Yer lost a little boy, eh?
HARRY. Next week, ain't it?
LEN. I got a shirt yer can do. (Laughs.) Any offers?
HARRY. She meet 'im?
LEN. Ain' arst.
HARRY. You?
LEN (shrugs). I'd 'ave t' get time off.
HARRY. Oh.
LEN. 'Ow d'yer get on at work?
HARRY (looks up). It's a job.
LEN. I meant with the blokes?
HARRY (irons). They're all right.

LEN. Funny, night work.

(PAM comes in. She has her hair in a towel. She carries a portable radio. Someone is talking. She sits on the couch and finds a pop program. She tunes in badly. She interrupts this from time to time to rub her hair.)

LEN (to HARRY). 'Ow about doin' my shirt? (He laughs. PAM finishes tuning. She looks around.)

PAM. 'Oo's got my *Radio Times*? You 'ad it? (HARRY does not answer. She turns to LEN.) You?

LEN (mumbles). Not again.

PAM. You speakin' t' me?

LEN. I'm sick t' death a yer bloody *Radio Times*.

PAM. Someone's 'ad it. (She rubs her hair vigorously.) I ain' goin' a get it no more. Not after last week. I'll cancel it. It's the last time I bring it in this 'ouse. I don't see why I 'ave t' go on paying for it. Yer must think I'm made a money. It's never 'ere when I wan'a see it. Not once. It's always the same. (She rubs her hair.) I notice no one else offers t' pay for it. Always Charlie. It's 'appened once too often this time.

LEN. Every bloody week the same!

PAM (to HARRY). Sure yer ain' got it?

HARRY. I bought this shirt over eight years ago.

PAM. That cost me sixpence a week. You reckon that up over a year. Yer must think I was born yesterday. (Pause. She rubs her hair.) Wasn't 'ere last week. Never 'ere. Got legs. (She goes to the door and shouts.) Mum! She 'eard all right. (She goes back to the couch and sits. She rubs her hair.) Someone's got it. I shouldn't think the people next door come in an' took it. Everyone 'as the benefit a it 'cept me. It's always the same. I'll know what t' do in future. Two can play at that game. I ain' blinkin' daft. (She rubs her hair.) I never begrudge no one borrowin' it, but yer'd think they'd have enough manners t' put it back. (Pause. She rubs her hair.) Juss walk all over yer. Well, it ain' goin' a 'appen again. They treat you like a door mat. All take and no give. Touch somethin' a their'n an' they go through the bloody ceilin'. It's bin the same ever since —

LEN. I tol' yer t' keep it in yer room!

PAM. Now yer got a lock things up in yer own 'ouse.

LEN. Why should we put up with this week after week juss because yer're too —

PAM. Yer know what yer can do.

LEN. Thass yer answer t' everythin'.

PAM. Got a better one?

HARRY. They was a pair first off. Set me back a quid each. Up the market. One's gone 'ome, went at the cuffs. Worth a quid.

LEN. Chriss. (Pause.)

PAM. I mean it this time. I'm goin' in that shop first thing Saturday mornin' an' tell 'im t' cancel it. I ain' throwin' my money down the drain juss to —

LEN. Wrap up!

PAM. Don't tell me what t' do!

LEN. Wrap up!

PAM. Thass typical a you. (She goes to the door and calls.) Mum! (To LEN.) I ain' stupid. I know 'oo's got it. (Calls.) Mum! — She can 'ear.

HARRY. Ain' worth readin' any'ow.

LEN. Don't start 'er off again.

PAM (to LEN). You ain' sittin' on it, a course!

LEN. No.

PAM. Yer ain' looked.

LEN. Ain' goin' to.

PAM. 'Ow d'yer know yer ain' sittin' on it?

LEN. I ain' sittin' on it.

PAM (to HARRY). Tell 'im t' get up!

HARRY. Waste a good money.

PAM (to LEN). Yer'll be sorry for this.

LEN. I'll be sorry for a lot a things.

HARRY. Cuffs goin' on this one.

PAM (by Len's chair). I ain' goin' till yer move.

HARRY. Lot a lies an' pictures a nancies.

PAM. Yer dead spiteful when yer wan'a be.

LEN. Thass right.

PAM (goes to the couch, rubbing her hair). 'E'oo laughs last. Fred's coming 'ome next week.

LEN. 'Ome?

PAM. 'Is ol' lady won't 'ave 'im in the 'ouse.

LEN. Where's 'e goin'?

PAM. Yer'll see.

LEN. 'E ain' 'avin' my room.

PAM. 'Oo said?

LEN. She won't let yer.

PAM. We'll see.

LEN. Yer ain' even arst 'er.

PAM. Oh, no?

LEN. No.

PAM (rubs her hair). We'll see.

LEN. I'll 'ave one or two things t' say. Yer too fond a pushin' people about.

PAM. Must take after you.

LEN. I thought 'e'd be sharin' your room.

PAM. I ain' rowin' about it. 'E'll 'ave t' 'ave somewhere t' come out to. Chriss knows what it's like shut up in them places. It'll be nice an' clean 'ere for 'im when yer're gone.

LEN. 'Ave yer arst 'im yet?

PAM. I ain' rowin' about it. If 'e goes wanderin' off 'e'll only end up in trouble again. I ain' goin' a be messed around over this! We ain' gettin' any younger. 'E's bound a be different. (She rubs her hair.) Yer can't say anythin' in letters. Yer can't expect 'im to.

LEN. 'Ave yer arst 'im?

PAM. I don' wan'a talk about it.

LEN. You meetin' 'im?

PAM. Why? — You ain' comin'!

LEN. 'Oo said?

PAM. 'E don't want you there!

LEN. 'Ow d'yer know?

PAM. Oh, let me alone!

LEN. 'E's my mate, ain' 'e?

PAM. I'm sick t' death a you under me feet all the time! Ain'
yer got no friends t' go to! What about yer people? Won't
they take yer in either?

LEN. Yer arst some stupid questions at times.

PAM. Yer can't 'ave no pride. Yer wouldn't catch me 'angin'
round where I ain' wanted.

LEN. 'Oo ain' wanted?

PAM. I don't want yer! They don't want yer! It's only common
sense! I don't know why yer can't see it. It's nothing' but
rows an' arguments.

LEN. 'Oo's fault's that?

PAM. Anybody else wouldn't stay if yer paid 'em! Yer caused
all the trouble last time.

LEN. I knew that was comin'.

PAM. None a that'd a 'appened if yer ain' bin 'ere. Yer never
give 'im a chance.

LEN. Yeh, yeh.

PAM. Yer live on trouble!

LEN. That ain' what 'e told everyone.

PAM. Same ol' lies.

LEN. Listen 'oo's talkin'!

PAM. Yer start off gettin' 'im put away —

LEN. Don't be bloody stupid!

PAM. Jealous! An' now 'e's comin' out yer still can't let 'im
alone!

LEN. *You* can't leave 'im alone, yer mean!

PAM. Yer laughed yer 'ead off when they took 'im away.

LEN. Bloody stupid! You arst 'im!

PAM. Comin' 'ere an' workin' me up!

LEN. Yer wan'a listen t' yerself!

PAM. So do you.

LEN. Shoutin'.

PAM. 'Oo's shoutin'?

LEN. You are!

PAM. Yer 'ave t' shout with you!

LEN. Thass right!

PAM. Yer so bloody dense!

LEN. Go on!

PAM. Yer 'ave t' shout!

LEN. Yer silly bloody cow!

PAM. Shoutin' 'e says! 'Ark at 'im! 'Ark at 'im!

LEN. Shut up!

PAM. We ain' carryin' on like this! Yer got a stop upsettin' me night after night!

LEN. You start it!

PAM. It's got a stop! It ain' worth it! Juss round an' round. (A very long silence.) Yer can't say it's the kid keepin' yer. (A long silence.) It certainly ain' me. Thass well past. (Silence.) Yer sit there in yer dirty ol' work clothes. (To HARRY.) Why don't yer turn 'im out? Dad.

HARRY. 'E pays 'is rent.

PAM. Fred'll pay.

HARRY. 'As 'e got a job?

PAM. 'E'll get one.

HARRY. Will 'e keep it?

PAM. Thass right!

LEN. Now 'oo's startin' it?

PAM. You are.

LEN. I ain' said a word.

PAM. No – but yer sat there!

LEN. I got some rights yer know!

PAM. Yer're juss like a kid.

LEN. I'm glad I ain' yourn.

PAM. I wouldn't like t' 'ave your spiteful nature.

LEN. I certainly wouldn't like yourn!

PAM. Thass right! I know why yer sittin' there!

LEN. Yer know a sight bloody too much!

PAM. I know where my *Radio Times* is!

LEN. Stick yer bloody *Radio Times*!

PAM. I know why yer sittin' there!

LEN. That bloody paper!

PAM. Why don't yer stand up?

LEN. Yer don't even want the bloody paper!

PAM. As long as yer causin' trouble —

LEN. Yer juss wan'a row!

PAM. — then yer're 'appy!

LEN. If yer found it yer'd lose somethin' else!

PAM (goes to Len's chair). Stand up then!

LEN. No!

PAM. Can't it a got there accidentally?

LEN. No!

PAM. Yer see!

LEN. I ain' bein' pushed around.

PAM. Yer see!

LEN. Yer come too much a it!

PAM. No, yer'd rather stay stuck!

LEN. A sight bloody too much!

PAM. An' row!

LEN. Shut up!

PAM. Thass right!

LEN. I tol' yer t' shut up!

PAM. Go on!

LEN. Or I'll bloody well shut yer up!

PAM. Oh, yeh!

LEN. Yer need a bloody good beltin'.

PAM. Touch me!

LEN. You started this!

PAM. Go on!

LEN (he turns away). Yer make me sick!

PAM. Yeh − yer see. Yer make me sick! (She goes to the door.) I ain' lettin' a bloody little weed like you push me around! (Calls.) Mum. (She comes back.) I wish I 'ad a record a when yer first come 'ere. Butter wouldn't melt in yer mouth. (Calls.) Mum!

HARRY (finishing ironing). Thass that, thank Chriss.

PAM (calls). Mum! − She can' 'ear. (Calls.) You 'eard?

HARRY. Put the wood in the 'ole.

LEN. I'd like t' 'ear what they're sayin' next door.

PAM. Let 'em say!

LEN. 'Ole bloody neighbor'ood must know!

PAM. Good − let 'em know what yer're like!

LEN. 'Oo wen' on about pride?

PAM (calls through door). I know yer can 'ear.

MARY (offstage). You callin', Pam?

PAM (to LEN). One thing, anythin' else goes wrong I'll know 'oo t' blame.

MARY (offstage). Pam!

PAM. Let 'er wait.

MARY (offstage). Pam!

LEN (calls). It's all right! One a 'er fits!

PAM (calls). 'E's sittin' on the chair.

MARY (offstage). What?

PAM (calls). 'E's got my paper!

MARY (offstage). What chair?

PAM (calls). 'E 'as!

MARY (offstage). I ain' got yer paper!

PAM (calls). It don't matter!

MARY (offstage). What paper's that?

PAM (calls). It don't matter! You bloody deaf?

LEN. Now start on 'er!

HARRY (piling his clothes neatly). Didn't take long.

PAM (to LEN). Yer're so bloody clever!

LEN. If I upset yer like this why don't *you* go?

PAM. Thass what you want!

LEN (shrugs). You want *me* t' go!

PAM. I ain' bein' pushed out on no streets.

LEN. I'm tryin' t' 'elp.

PAM. Yer wouldn't 'elp a cryin' baby.

LEN. Yer're the last one a bring that up!

PAM. 'Elp? – after the way yer carried on t'night.

LEN. I lost me job stayin' out a 'elp you when yer was sick!

PAM. Sacked for bein' bloody lazy!

LEN (stands). Satisfied?

PAM (without looking at the chair). Yer torn it up or burnt it! Wouldn't put that pass yer! (She goes out. Silence. HARRY finishes folding his clothes.)

MARY (offstage). Found it yet? (Pause.)

HARRY. Wan'a use it?

LEN. No. (HARRY folds the board.)

SCENE NINE

The living room. LEN has spread a paper on the floor. He cleans his shoes on it. MARY comes in. She is in her slip. She walks about getting ready.

MARY. 'Ope yer don't mind me like this.

LEN. You kiddin'?

MARY. It's such a rush. I don't really wan'a go.

LEN. Don't then.

MARY. I said I would now.

LEN. Say yer don't feel up to it.

MARY. Yes. (She goes on getting ready.) Makes a change I suppose.

LEN. Never know, it might be a laugh.

MARY. Yer got a do somethin' t' entertain yerself. (Pause.) I 'ope yer ain' usin' 'er *Radio Times*.

LEN. Ha!

MARY. She's got no patience. It'll land 'er in trouble one a these days. Look at that pram. I told 'er t' wait. She should a got two 'undred for that.

LEN. Easy.

MARY (looks at her shoes). This ain' nice. No, she 'as t' let it go for fifty quid, the first time she's arst. Can't be told. Yer couldn't give these a little touch up for me?

LEN. Sling 'em over.

MARY. Ta, dear.

LEN. What yer put on these?

MARY. That white stuff. (LEN polishes her shoes in silence.) Thinkin'?

LEN. No.

MARY. Whass worryin' yer?

LEN. Nothin'.

MARY. I expect yer're like me. Yer enjoy the quiet. I don't enjoy all this noise yer get.

LEN. She said somethin' about my room?

MARY (amused). Why?

LEN. What she say?

MARY. That worried yer?

LEN. I ain' worried.

MARY. She's not tellin' me 'ow t' run my 'ouse. (She pulls on her stockings.)

LEN. Oh. (Holds up her shoes.) Do yer?

MARY. Very nice. Juss go over the backs, dear. I like t' feel nice be'ind. I tol' 'er there's enough t' put up with without lookin' for trouble.

LEN. Better?

MARY. Yes. I 'ad enough a that pair last time. (She steps into one shoe.) We're only goin' for the big film. She can do what she likes outside.

LEN (gives her the other shoe). Thass yer lot.

MARY. 'E wants lockin' up for life. Ta, dear. I don't expect
yer t' understand at your age, but things don't turn out too
bad. There's always someone worse off in the world.

LEN (clearing up the polishing things). Yer can always be that
one.

MARY. She's my own flesh an' blood, but she don't take after
me. Not a thought in 'er 'ead. She's 'ad a rough time a it.
I feel sorry for 'er about the kid –

LEN. One a them things. Yer can't make too much a it.

MARY. Never 'ave 'appened if she'd a look after it right. Yer
done a lovely job on these. What yer doin' t'night?

LEN (sews a button on his shirt). Gettin' ready for work.

MARY. Yer don't go out so much.

LEN. I was out Tuesday.

MARY. Yer ought a be out every night.

LEN. Can't afford it.

MARY. There's plenty a nice girls round 'ere.

LEN. I ain' got the energy these days. They want – somethin'
flash.

MARY. Yer can't tell me what they want. I was the same that
age.

LEN. I ain' got time for 'alf a 'em. They don't know what
they got it for.

MARY. I thought that's what you men were after.

LEN. 'Alf a 'em, it ain' worth the bother a gettin' there. Thass
a fact.

MARY. What about the other 'alf?

LEN. Hm!

MARY (having trouble with her suspender). Yer 'ave t' go about
it the right way. Yer can't stand a girl in a puddle down the
back a some ol' alley an' think yer doin' 'er a favor. Yer
got yer own room upstairs. That's a nice room. Surprised
yer don't use that. I don't mind what goes on, yer know that.

As long as yer keep the noise down.

LEN. Ta.

MARY. It's in every man. It 'as t' come out. (Pause.) We didn't carry on like that when I was your age.

LEN. Pull the other one.

MARY. Not till yer was in church. Anyway, yer 'ad t' be engaged. I think it's nicer in the open. I do.

LEN. I bet yer bin up a few alleys.

MARY. You enjoy yerself. I know what I'd be doin' if I was you.

LEN. You meetin' a fella?

MARY. No! I'm goin' out with Mrs. Lee.

LEN. Waste.

MARY. Don't be cheeky.

LEN. Yer look fair when yer all done up.

MARY. What you after? Bin spendin' me rent money?

LEN. Wass on?

MARY. Don't know. Somethin' daft.

LEN. Shall I look it up?

MARY. They're all the same. Sex. Girls 'angin' out a their dresses an' men bendin' over 'em.

LEN. It's one of them nudes. 'Eard the fellas talkin'.

MARY. Shan't go in.

LEN. Don't know what yer missin'.

MARY. Different for men.

LEN. Always full a tarts when I bin.

MARY. Thass where yer spend yer money.

LEN. Very nice. Big ol' tits bouncin' about in sinner-scope.

MARY. Don't think Mrs. Lee'd fancy that.

LEN. I'll 'ave t' take yer one a these nights.

MARY. I'd rather see Tarzan.

LEN. Thass easy, come up next time I 'ave a bath.

MARY. Count the 'airs on yer chest?

LEN. For a start.

MARY. Sounds like a 'orror film.

LEN. I enjoy a good scrub. On me back.

MARY. Thass the regular carry-on in China.

LEN. No 'arm in it.

MARY. No. (Slight pause.) Pam's very easy goin' for a nice girl. I suppose yer miss that.

LEN. Takes a bit a gettin' used to.

MARY. 'Ow'd yer manage?

LEN. Any suggestions? (Slight pause.)

MARY. Bugger!

LEN. Eh?

MARY. Thass tore it!

LEN. Wass up?

MARY. Oh, blast! I caught me stockin'.

LEN. Oh.

MARY. That would 'ave to 'appen.

LEN. 'Ow'd yer do it?

MARY. Juss when I'm late. Bugger it. (She looks in the table drawer.) 'Ardly worth goin' in a minute. Excuse my language. Never find anythin' when yer want it in this place.

LEN. What yer lost?

MARY. It's the only decent pair I got.

LEN. Thass a shame.

MARY. It'll run.

LEN. Less 'ave a shufties.

MARY. Caught on that blasted chair. It's bin like that for ages.

LEN. Yeh. Thass a big one.

MARY. Pam's got 'er nail varnish all over the place except when yer wan'a find it.

LEN (offers her the needle). 'Ave a loan of this.

MARY. It'll run, y'see.

LEN. Less do the cotton.

MARY. I certainly can't afford new ones this week.

LEN (threading the needle). Not t'worry.

MARY. I'm no good at that.

LEN. Well, 'ave a bash.

MARY. It'll make it worse.

LEN. No it won't.

MARY (puts her foot on the chair seat). You do it.

LEN. Me?

MARY. I never could use a needle. I should a bin there by now.

LEN. I don't know if I —

MARY. Get on. It's only doin' me a good turn.

LEN. It ain' that. I —

MARY. Mrs. Lee's waitin'. I can't take 'em off. I'm in ever such a 'urry. They'll run.

LEN. Yeh. It's dodgy. I don't wan'a prick —

MARY. Yer got steady 'ands your age. (LEN kneels in front of her and starts darning.)

LEN. Yeh. (He drops the needle.) Oh.

MARY. All right?

LEN. It's dropped.

MARY. What?

LEN. Me needle.

MARY. Yer're 'oldin' me up.

LEN (on his hands and knees). 'Ang on.

MARY. That it?

LEN. No.

MARY (helps him to look). Can't a got far.

LEN. It's gone.

MARY. What's that?

LEN. Where?

MARY. That's it. There.

LEN. Oh. Ta.

MARY (puts her foot back on the chair). I ain' got all night.

LEN. I'll 'ave to get me 'and inside.

MARY. You watch where yer go. Yer ain' on yer 'oneymoon yet. Yer 'and's cold!

LEN. Keep still, or it'll jab yer.

MARY. You watch yerself.

LEN. I'll juss give it a little stretch.

MARY. All right?

LEN. Yer got lovely legs.

MARY. You get on with it.

LEN. Lovely an' smooth.

MARY. Never mind my legs.

LEN. It's a fact.

MARY. Some people'd 'ave a fit if they 'eard that. Yer know what they're like.

LEN. Frustrated.

MARY. I'm old enough t' be yer mother.

(HARRY comes in. He goes straight to the table.)

MARY (to LEN). Go steady!

LEN. Sorry.

MARY. You watch where yer pokin'. That 'urt.

LEN. I tol' yer t' keep still.

MARY. Yer'll make it bigger, not smaller. (HARRY takes ink and a Pools coupon from the table drawer. He puts them on the table.)

LEN. That'll see yer through t'night. (He ties a knot in the thread.)

MARY. Wass up now?

LEN. Scissors.

MARY. Eh?

LEN. I 'ad 'em juss now.

MARY. Bite it.

LEN. Eh?

MARY. Go on.

LEN (leans forward). Keep still.

MARY. I can't wait all night. (LEN bites the thread off. HARRY goes out.) Took yer time.

LEN (stands). Ow! I'm stiff.

MARY (looks). Ta, very nice.

LEN. Ain' worth goin' now.

MARY. 'Ave I got me cigarettes?

LEN. Might be somethin' on telly.

MARY. I can't disappoint Mrs. Lee.

LEN. I 'ad a feelin' 'e'd come in.

MARY. Yer'll be in bed time I get back.

LEN. She won't wait this long.

MARY. I'll say good night. Thanks for 'elpin'.

LEN. Stay in an' put yer feet up. I'll make us a cup of tea.

MARY. Can't let yer friends down. Cheerio.

LEN. Okay. (MARY goes. LEN takes a handkerchief from his pocket. He switches the light off and goes to the couch.)

SCENE TEN

A cafe. Furniture: Chairs and three tables, one up right, one right and one down left. Apart from this the stage is bare. LEN and PAM sit at the table up right.

LEN (drinks tea). Warms yer up. (Pause.) These early mornin's knock me out. 'Nother cup? (Pause.)

PAM. Wass the time?

LEN. Quarter past.

PAM. Why ain't they got a clock? (Pause.)

LEN. 'Ave another one.

PAM. Thass the fourth time yer keep arstin'.

LEN. Warm yer up.

PAM. Go an' sit on yer own table. (Pause.)

LEN. Sure yer wrote the name right?

PAM. We'll look bloody daft when 'e finds you 'ere. Wass 'e goin' to say?

LEN. 'Ello. (Pause.) Let me go an' find 'im.

PAM. No.

LEN. There's no use —

PAM. No!

LEN. Suit yerself.

PAM. Do I 'ave t' say everythin' twice?

LEN. There's no need t' shout.

PAM. I ain' shoutin'.

LEN. They can 'ear yer 'alf way t' —

PAM. I don't wan'a know.

LEN. Yer never do. (Silence.)

PAM. Len. I don't want a keep on at yer. I don't know what's the matter with me. They wan'a put the 'eat on. It's like death. Yer'd get on a lot better with someone else.

LEN. Per'aps 'e ain' comin'.

PAM. They must 'ave all the winders open. It's no life for a fella. Yer ain' a bad sort.

LEN. Yeh. I'm goin' a be late in.

PAM. Don't go.

LEN. You make me money up?

PAM (after a slight pause). Why can't yer go somewhere?

LEN. Where?

PAM. There's lots a places.

LEN. Easy t' say.

PAM. I'll find yer somewhere.

LEN. I ain' scuttlin' off juss t' make room for you t' shag in.

PAM. Yer're a stubborn sod! Don't blame me what 'appens t' yer! Yer ain' messin' me about again.

LEN. I knew that wouldn't last long!

PAM. I'm sick t' death a yer. Clear off! (She goes to the table down left and sits. LEN goes out left. Pause. He comes back with a cup of tea. He puts it on the table in front of PAM. He stands near the table.)

LEN. It'll get cold. (Pause.) Did 'e say 'e'd come? (Pause.) Did 'e answer any a your letters? (She reacts.) I juss wondered!

PAM. I tol' yer before!

LEN. Thass all right then. (Pause.)

PAM. It's like winter in 'ere.

(There are voices off right. Someone shouts. A door bangs
    open. MIKE, COLIN, PETE, BARRY, FRED and LIZ come
    in.)

COLIN. 'Ere we are again.
BARRY. Wipe yer boots.
MIKE. On you!
BARRY. Where we sittin'?
MIKE. On yer 'ead.
BARRY. On me arse!
LIZ. Don't know 'ow 'e tells the difference. (She laughs.)
FRED. This'll do.
PETE. All right?
LIZ. Can I sit 'ere?
MIKE. Sit where yer like, dear.
BARRY. What we 'avin'?
PETE (to FRED). What yer fancy?
FRED. What they got?
PETE (looks left). Double egg, bacon, 'am, bangers, double
    bangers, sper-gety —
BARRY. Chips.
FRED. Juss bring the lot.
PETE. Oi, ease off.
FRED. An' four cups a tea.
PETE. I'm standin' yer for this!
FRED. Make that twice.
BARRY. An' me!
PETE (to LIZ). Wass yourn, darlin'?
FRED. Now or later?
PETE. Now, t' start with.
BARRY. Tea and crumpet.
LIZ. Could I 'ave a coffee?
FRED. 'Ave what yer like, darlin'.

BARRY. Cup a tea do me!

COLIN. Wass she 'avin' later!

LIZ. Dinner.

MIKE. Teas all round then.

BARRY. Right.

MIKE (to FRED). Sit down, we'll fix it. (PETE, MIKE and COLIN go off left.)

FRED. Where's all the burn?

LIZ. I only got one left.

FRED (calls). Get us some snout.

MIKE. Five or ten? (FRED makes a rude gesture. LIZ offers him her cigarette.)

FRED. Keep it, darlin'. I'm okay. (He turns to LEN and PAM. Oi, 'ello then. 'Ow's it goin'? (He stands and goes down to their table. LEN has already sat.)

PAM. 'Ello.

FRED. Thass right, yer said yer'd be 'ere. (Calls.) That grub ready? (To PAM.) Yeh.

BARRY (to FRED). Big gut!

COLIN (offstage). Give us a chance!

PETE (offstage). They didn't teach yer no manners inside.

FRED. Yer're arstin' for trouble. I don't wan'a go back juss yet.

PAM. You all right?

FRED. Yeh. You look all right.

LIZ. Don't yer reckon 'e looks thin?

PAM. I can't —

LIZ. Like a rake. I tol' yer, didn't I? Yer wan'a get some meat on yer.

FRED. I will when that grub turns up. (BARRY and LIZ are sitting at the table up right. BARRY bangs the table.)

BARRY. Grub!

COLIN (offstage). Ease up, louse!

BARRY (calls). Make that two coffees. (He puts on an accent.) I feel like a cup.

LIZ. Ain' what yer sound like.

PETE (offstage). Shut 'im up! (BARRY makes a gesture.)

FRED. Why did the policewoman marry the 'angman?

LIZ. Eh?

FRED. They both liked necking. (They laugh.)

PETE (offstage). Why was the undertaker buried alive?

LIZ. 'Is job got on top a 'im. (They laugh.)

BARRY. Why did the woman with three tits 'ave quads?

MIKE. We 'eard it! (The rest groan.)

COLIN (offstage). What about the sailor 'oo drowned in 'is bath?

FRED. 'Is brother was the fireman 'oo went up in smoke. (They laugh.)

PETE (offstage). Didn't know they let yer 'ave jokes inside.

LIZ. Wass it like?

FRED. In there?

LIZ. Yeh.

FRED (shrugs; to LEN). 'Ow's the job?

LEN. Stinks.

FRED. It don't change. (He sits at their table.) Long time.

LIZ. Got a light?

FRED (to PAM). I got yer letters, didn't I?

PAM. Yeh.

FRED. I ain' good at writin'. (PETE, COLIN and MIKE shout and laugh, off.)

PAM. Where yer goin'?

FRED. I'm goin' to 'ave the biggest nosh-up a me life.

BARRY (to FRED). Did yer be'ave yerself inside?

PAM (to FRED). No, after that.

FRED. Oh, yer know.

PAM. Yer fixed up?

FRED. 'Ow?

PAM. I'll take yer roun' our place.

FRED. Oh –

LEN. Yer can muck in with me a couple a nights. Give yerself time t' get straight.

FRED. Ta, I don't wan' a put —

LEN. Yer won't be in the way for a couple of days.

PAM. Mum'll shut up. It'll be nice and quiet. Thass what yer need.

FRED. Yer must be kidding!

BARRY (to LIZ). Arst 'im if 'e be'aved isself.

LIZ (to FRED). 'Ear that?

FRED. Yer know me.

BARRY. Not 'arf.

FRED. One day.

LIZ. Yeh.

FRED. This padre 'as me in.

BARRY. Oh, yeah.

FRED. Wants t' chat me up. 'E says nothin' that comes out a a man can be all bad.

BARRY. Whass that?

FRED. Then 'e 'ops out an' I 'as a little slash in 'is tea. (LIZ and BARRY laugh — LIZ very loudly.)

LIZ. What 'appened?

FRED. 'E reckoned they ain' put the sugar in. (They laugh.) Another bloke —

LIZ. Yeh.

FRED. Stares at me. Keeps starin' at me. All day. It's 'is first day, see.

BARRY. Go on.

FRED. So I gets 'im on the landin' an' clobbers 'im.

BARRY. Bang!

FRED. An' it only turns out 'e'd got a squint! (They laugh.)

LIZ. Wass it like inside?

FRED. I got chokey for the clobberin'. Bread and water!

BARRY. On yer jack.

FRED. Only good thing there's no one t' scrounge yer grub.

BARRY. Yer d'narf tell 'em.

FRED. Ain' my sort a life. Glad I done it once, but thass their

    lot. Ain' pinnin' nothin' on me next time.
LIZ. Wass it like?
FRED. In there?
LIZ. Yeh.
FRED. Cold.
LIZ. Eh?
FRED. Cold. (Silence.)

(MIKE comes in a few paces from the left.)

MIKE. Won't be 'alf a jik.
FRED. 'Bout time.
COLIN (offstage). 'E still moanin'?

(COLIN comes on and stands with MIKE.)

FRED. Eh?
COLIN. Bet yer couldn't carry-on in there.
FRED. Lot I couldn't do in there, if yer like t' look at it.
MIKE. We ain' got a treat yer everyday.
FRED. I'll pay for this if you like. (To LIZ.) Lend us ten bob.

(PETE comes in.)

PETE. 'Oo arst yer t' pay?
FRED. I reckon it's worth one lousy meal.
PETE. Yer made yer own decisions, didn't yer?
BARRY (comes down). Wass up?
PETE. We ain' got a crawl up yer arse.
COLIN. Grub smell all right, don't —
PETE. 'Ang on a minute, Col.
MIKE (to PETE). Nah, it's 'is first day out, Pete. Let 'im settle
    down.
COLIN. Come on. (He starts to go left.)
PETE. 'E ain' swingin' that one on me. (PETE and COLIN

go out left.)

MIKE (to FRED). 'E got out the wrong bed this mornin'. (MIKE follows them off. Slight pause.)

FRED (laughs). It's the ol' lag comin' out a me! (Shouts.) Whoopee!

BARRY. Ha-ha! Whoopee!

FRED.

> She was only a goalkeeper's daughter
>
> She married a player called Jack
>
> It was great when 'e played center forward
>
> But 'e liked to slip round to the back.

(He laughs.). I used a lie in me pit thinkin' a that.

COLIN (offstage). What?

FRED. Nosh.

LIZ. That all?

FRED. An' tryin' a remember whass up your legs.

LIZ. I'll draw yer a picture. Give us a light.

FRED (to PAM). Give 'er a light. (He gives PAM a box of matches. She takes them to LIZ. To LEN.) Wass 'er game?

LEN. I don't wan'a get involved, mate.

FRED. Yeh? Yer should a read them crummy letters she keeps sendin'. She ain' goin' a catch me round 'er place.

LEN. No. What was it like?

FRED. No, talk about somethin' else.

LEN. No, *before*.

FRED. Yer 'eard the trial. (PAM comes back to the table.) Go away, Pam.

PAM. I wan'a finish me tea.

LEN. Thass cold.

FRED. Can't yer take a 'int? Take yer tea over there.

PAM. Wass goin' on?

LEN. Nothin'!

FRED. No one's talkin' about you.

PAM (going to sit down at the table). I'd rather —

FRED. Oh, Pam! (She goes to the unoccupied table and watches them.) 'Er ol' people still alive? If yer can call it that.

LEN. Yeh.

FRED. Yer ain' still livin' there?

LEN. I'm goin' soon.

FRED. Yer're as bad as them. She won't get me there in a
month a Sundays.

LEN. What was it like?

FRED. I tol' yer.

LEN. No, before.

FRED. Before what?

LEN. In the park.

FRED. Yer saw.

LEN. Wass it feel like?

FRED. Don't know.

LEN. When yer was killin' it.

FRED. Do what?

LEN. Wass it feel like when yer killed it?

BARRY (to LIZ). Fancy a record?

LIZ. Wouldn't mind.

BARRY. Give us a tanner then.

LIZ. Yer're as tight as a flea's arse'ole.

BARRY. An 'alf as 'andsome. I know. – Out a change. (LIZ
gives him sixpence. He goes off down right.)

(MIKE brings on two cups.)

MIKE. Comin' up.

FRED. Very 'andy.

BARRY (offstage). 'Ow about "I Broke My 'Eart"?

LIZ. Yeh. Thass great.

BARRY (offstage). Well, they ain' got it.

LIZ. Funny! What about "My 'Eart Is Broken"?

MIKE (to LIZ). One coffee.

BARRY (offstage). They got that.

LIZ (to MIKE). The sugar in it?

MIKE. Taste it. (MIKE goes off left.)
LEN. Whass it like, Fred?
FRED (drinks). It ain' like this in there.
LEN. Fred.
FRED. I tol' yer.
LEN. No yer ain'.
FRED. I forget.
LEN. I thought yer'd a bin full a it. I was —
FRED. Len!
LEN. — curious, thass all, 'ow it feels t' —
FRED. No! (He slams his fist on the table.)
LEN. Okay.
FRED. It's finished.
LEN. Yeh.
FRED (stands). What yer wan'a do? (The juke box starts.)
LEN. Nothin'.
FRED. Wass 'e gettin' at?
LEN. It's finished.

(PETE, MIKE, COLIN and BARRY come in. PAM stands.
    LIZ still sits.)

FRED. I were'n'the only one.
LEN. I ain' gettin' at yer, skip.
PETE. Wass up?
FRED. Nothin' a do with you.
PAM. 'E was rowin'.
FRED. It's nothin'. Where's that grub?
PAM. I knew 'e'd start somethin'.
FRED. Forget it.
PAM. I tol' 'im not t' come.
FRED. Where's that flippin' grub? Move. (COLIN and MIKE
    go off left.)
PAM. 'E won't let me alone.
FRED. I'm starvin', I know that.

PAM. 'E follers me everywhere.

FRED. Ain' you lucky.

PAM. Tell 'im for me! 'It 'im! 'It 'im!

FRED. It's nothin' a do with me!

PAM. It is! It is!

BARRY. She's started.

FRED. 'Ere we go! (He sits and puts his head in his hands.)

PAM (to LEN). See what yer done?

FRED. Didn't take 'er long.

PAM. It's your place t' stick up for me, love. I went through all that trouble for you! Somebody's got a save me from 'im.

FRED. Thanks. Thanks very much. I'll remember this. (He stands and starts back to his own table.)

LIZ (starting to click her fingers). I can't 'ear the music!

PAM (to LEN). Don't bloody sit there! Yer done enough 'arm!

PETE. 'Oo brought 'er 'ere?

FRED. Chriss knows!

PAM (pointing to LEN). 'E started this!

FRED. I don't care what bleedin' wet started it. You can stop it!

PAM (to LEN). I 'ate yer for this!

FRED. *Belt up*!

PAM (goes to FRED, who sits at his table). I'm sorry. Fred, 'e's goin' now. It'll be all right when 'e's gone. (LEN does not move.)

FRED. All right.

PAM (looks around). Where's 'is grub? 'E's starvin' 'ere. (She goes to touch his arm.) I get so worked up when 'e —

FRED. Keep yer 'ands off me! So 'elp me I'll land yer so bloody 'ard they'll put me back for life!

PETE (moving in). Right. Less get ourselves sorted out.

(COLIN comes on left.)

PAM. It don't matter. I juss got excited. (Calls.) Where's 'is breakfast? It'll be time for —

FRED. Breakfast? I couldn't eat in this bloody place if they served it through a rubber tube.

PETE. Come on! (Calls.) Mike!

FRED. All I done for 'er an' she 'as the bloody nerve t' start this!

PETE. Come on, less move.

BARRY. She wants throttlin'.

(MIKE comes on left. COLIN and FRED go out right. The door bangs.)

LIZ. I ain' drunk me coffee.

PETE. I said move!

MIKE. Flippin' mad'ouse. (He goes out right. The door bangs.)

LIZ. We paid for it!

PETE. Move! (LIZ and BARRY go out right. The door bangs.) You come near 'im again an' I'll settle yer for good. Lay off. (He goes out right. The door bangs. LEN still sits. PAM stands. Pause.)

LEN. I'll see yer 'ome. I'm late for work already. I know I'm in the way. Yer can't go round the streets when yer're like that. (He hesitates.) They ain' done 'im no good. 'E's gone back like a kid. Yer well out a it. (He stands.) I knew the little bleeder'ld do a bunk! Can't we try an' get on like before? (He looks around.) There's no one else. Yer only live once.

SCENE ELEVEN

The living room. On the table: bread, butter, breadknife, cup and saucer and milk. MARY sits on the couch. HARRY comes in with a pot of tea. He goes to the table. He cuts and

butters bread.   Pauses while he works.   MARY goes out.
HARRY goes on working.   MARY comes back with a cup
and saucer. She pours herself tea. She takes it to the couch
and sits. She sips. HARRY moves so that his back is to her.
He puts his cup upright in his saucer. He puts milk in the cup.
He reaches to pick up the teapot. MARY stands, goes to the
table, and moves the teapot out of his reach. She goes back
to the couch. Sits. Sips.

MARY. My teapot. (Sips. Pause.)
HARRY. My tea. (He pours tea into his cup. MARY stands and
     goes to the table. She empties his cup on the floor.) Our'n.
     Weddin' present.
MARY (goes to the couch and sits). From *my* mother.
HARRY. That was joint.
MARY.   Don't you dare talk to me!   (HARRY goes out.
     Loudly.) Some minds want boilin' in carbolic. Soap's too
     good for 'em. (Slight pause.) Dirty filth! Worse! Ha! (She
     goes to the door and calls.) Don't you dare talk to me!

(MARY goes to the couch and sits. HARRY comes in.)

HARRY. I'll juss say one word. I saw yer with yer skirt up.
     Yer call me filth? (He goes out. Slight pause. MARY goes
     to the table and empties his slices of bread onto the floor.
     She goes back to the couch and drinks her tea.)
MARY. Mind out of a drain! I wouldn't let a kid like that touch
     me if 'e paid for it!

(HARRY comes in. He goes straight to the table.)

HARRY. I don't want to listen.
MARY. Filth!
HARRY.   There's bin enough trouble in this 'ouse. Now yer
     wan'a cause trouble with 'im!

MARY. Don't talk t' me! You!

HARRY (sees his bread on the floor). Yer juss wan'a start trouble like there was before! (He stoops and picks up the bread.) Middle-age woman — goin' with 'er own daughter's left-overs — 'alf 'er age — makin' 'erself a spectacle — look at this! — No self control.

MARY. Filth!

HARRY. Like a child — I pity the lad — must want 'is 'ead tested.

MARY. There'll be some changes in this 'ouse. I ain' puttin' up with this after t'day. Yer can leave my things alone for a start. All this stuff come out a my pocket. I worked for it! I ain' 'avin' you dirtyin' me kitchin. Yer can get yerself some new towels for a start! An' plates! An' knives! An' cups! Yer'll soon find a difference!

HARRY. Don't threaten me —

MARY. An' my cooker! An' my curtains! An' my sheets!

HARRY. Yer'll say somethin' yer'll be sorry for! (He comes toward her. There is a chair in the way. He trips over it. The leg comes off.)

MARY. Don't you touch me!

HARRY. Two can play at your game! Yeh! I can stop your money t'morra!

MARY. Don't yer raise yer 'and t' me! (HARRY goes back to the table. He starts cutting bread. Pause.) I knew yer was stood outside when 'e was there. I 'eard yer through the door. I'd a bet my life you'd come in!

HARRY. Old enough t' be 'is mother. Yer must be 'ard up!

MARY. I seen you stuck 'ere long enough! You couldn't pick an' choose!

HARRY. One was enough.

MARY. No one else would a put up with yer!

HARRY. I can do without! Yer ain' worth it!

MARY. Ha! I saw yer face when yer come through that door. I bin watchin' yer all the week. I know you of old, Harry!

HARRY. Yer'll go out a yer mind one day!

MARY. Filth!

HARRY. I 'ad enough a you in the past! I ain' puttin' up with your lark again. I'm too old. I wan' a bit a peace an' quiet.

MARY. Then why did yer come in?

HARRY. Me pools was in that table.

MARY. Yer was spyin'! Yer bin sniffin' round ever since! I ain' puttin' up with your dirt! (She picks up the teapot.) Yer can bloody well stay in yer room!

(PAM comes in.)

PAM. Chriss. (Calls.) It's them!

HARRY (cutting bread). I ain' sunk so low I'll bother *you*!

MARY. Yer jealous ol' swine!

HARRY. Of a bag like you?

MARY. 'E don't think so! I could a gone t'bed, an' I will next tme 'e arsts me!

HARRY. Now 'e's caught a sniff a yer 'e'll be off with 'is tail between 'is legs! (She hits him with the teapot. The water pours over him. PAM is too frightened to move.) Ah!

MARY. 'Ope yer die!

HARRY. Blood!

MARY. Use words t' me!

HARRY. Blood!

PAM. Mum!

HARRY. Ah!

LEN (offstage). Whass up?

HARRY. Doctor.

MARY. Cracked me weddin' present. 'Im.

(LEN comes in.)

LEN. Blimey!

HARRY. Scalded!

PAM. Whass 'appenin'?

HARRY. She tried t' murder me!

MARY. Yer little liar!

PAM. Are yer all right?

HARRY. Yer saw 'er.

MARY. 'E went mad.

LEN. It's only a scratch.

PAM (to MARY). Why?

MARY. 'Effin' and' blindin'.

LEN' Yer'll live.

HARRY. Blood.

PAM (to MARY). Whass 'e done?

LEN. 'E's all wet.

MARY. Swore at me!

PAM. Why?

HARRY. Doctor.

MARY. There's nothin' wrong with 'im.

HARRY. Scalded.

MARY. I 'ardly touched 'im. 'E needs a good thrashin'!

LEN (to PAM). Get a towel.

HARRY. I ain' allowed t' touch the towels.

MARY. I kep' this twenty-three years. Look what 'e's done to it!

PAM. *What 'appened*?

LEN. Nothin'. They 'ad a row.

PAM. 'E called 'er a bag.

LEN. It's nothin'. I'd better be off t' work. They'll give us me cards. We juss seen Fred. 'E looks all right, well, 'e don't look bad. It ain' Butlins. (To PAM.) Get 'im up t' bed. Put the kettle on. Yer could all do with a cup a tea.

PAM (to MARY). What made yer start talkin'?

MARY. Yer 'eard 'im call me a bag. (To LEN.) 'E went mad over catchin' you last week.

LEN (looking at Harry's head). Yer'll 'ave t' wash that cut. It's got tealeaves in it. (HARRY dabs at it with the tail of his shirt.)

PAM. Caught 'oo last week?

MARY (pointing to HARRY). 'Is filth. (Points to LEN.) Arst 'im!

PAM (to LEN). What 'appened?

LEN. Nothin'.

HARRY. I was cuttin' bread. (He picks up the knife.) She flew at me!

PAM (to LEN). I knew it was you! (To HARRY.) Whass 'e done?

LEN. Nothin'.

MARY. Filth!

HARRY. I found 'em both. (He points with the knife to the spot.)

LEN (pulling at HARRY). No!

HARRY. She'll 'ave t' 'ear.

LEN (he pulls at him). No!

HARRY. She 'ad 'er clothes up.

PAM. No!

LEN. Yer bloody fool! Yer bloody, bloody fool! (He shakes HARRY. The knife waves through the air.)

HARRY. Ah!

PAM. That knife!

MARY. Filth!

PAM. 'E'll kill 'im!

LEN. Bloody fool.

PAM (screams). Oh! No! – Whass 'appenin' to us? (She sits on the couch and cries. Pause.)

HARRY. 'Im an' 'er.

PAM (crying). Why don't 'e go? Why don't 'e go away? All my friends gone. Baby's gone. Nothin' left but rows. Day in, day out. Fightin' with knives.

HARRY. I'm shakin'.

PAM (crying). They'll kill each other soon.

LEN (to PAM). Yer can't blame them on me!

PAM (crying). Why can't 'e go away!

HARRY (removes his shirt). Wet.

PAM (crying). Look at me. I can't sleep with worry.

MARY. Breakin' me 'ome.

PAM (crying). 'E's killed me baby. Taken me friends. Broken me 'ome.

HARRY. More blood.

MARY. I ain' clearin' up after 'im. 'E can clear 'is own mess.

PAM (crying). I can't go on like this.

LEN (to PAM). There was nothin' in it!

PAM (crying). I'll throw myself somewhere. It's the only way.

HARRY. Cold. (LEN goes to HARRY.)

PAM (sitting and crying). Stop 'im! They'll kill each other!

LEN (stops). I was goin' a 'elp 'im.

PAM (crying). Take that knife. The baby's dead. They're all gone. It's the only way. I can't go on.

MARY. Next time 'e won't be so lucky.

PAM (crying). Yer can't call it livin'. 'E's pullin' me t' pieces. Nothin' but trouble.

LEN. I'm tryin' t' 'elp! 'Oo else'll 'elp? If I go will they come back? Will the baby come back? Will 'e come back? I'm the only one that's stayed an' yer wan'a get rid a me!

PAM (crying). I can't stand any more. Baby dead. No friends.

LEN. I'll go.

PAM (crying). No one listens. Why don't 'e go? Why don't they make 'im go?

MARY. 'E can stay in 'is own room after t'day.

LEN. I'll find somewhere dinnertime.

HARRY. Me neck's throbbin'.

PAM (crying). No 'ome. No friends. Baby dead. Gone. Fred gone.

SCENE TWELVE

Len's bedroom. LEN lies face down on the floor. The side of his face is flat against the floorboards. He holds a knife. There is an open suitcase on the bed. In it are a few things. Pause. The door opens. HARRY comes in. He wears long white combinations. He wears pale socks. No shoes. His head is in a skull cap of bandages. He comes up behind LEN. LEN sees him slowly.

HARRY. Evenin'.

LEN. Evenin'.

HARRY. Get up. Yer'll catch cold down there.

LEN. 'Ow's yer 'ead?

HARRY (touches it). Don't know.

LEN. Thass a good sign.

HARRY. All right now?

LEN. I was listenin'. (He draws the knife between two boards.) Clears the crack. Yer can 'ear better.

HARRY. Thass a good knife.

LEN. She's got someone with 'er.

HARRY. Thought yer might like someone t' say good night.

LEN. Yer can 'ear 'er voice.

HARRY. No.

LEN. She's picked someone up. I couldn't get anywhere with me packin'.

HARRY. No, I saw 'er come in.

LEN. Could a swore I 'eard someone.

HARRY. Not with 'er!

LEN. She's still good lookin'.

HARRY. 'Er sort's two a penny. Lads don't 'ave t' put up with 'er carry-on.

LEN. I used t' 'ear Fred an' her down there.

HARRY. No more.

LEN. Kep' me awake.

HARRY (sits on the bed). Tired. Nice 'ere.

LEN. Seen worse.

HARRY. Quiet.

LEN. Sometimes. (Pause.)

HARRY. She's cryin'.

LEN. Oh.

HARRY. In bed. I passed 'er door.

LEN. I knew I 'eard somethin'.

HARRY. Thass what yer 'eard. (LEN puts a pair of socks in the case.) Won't be the last time.

LEN. Eh?

HARRY. 'Owlin' in bed.

LEN. Oh.

HARRY. She'll pay for it.

LEN. What?

HARRY. 'Er ways. Yer'll get yer own back.

LEN. I lost me case keys.

HARRY. Yer'll see.

LEN. Long time since I used it.

HARRY. Where yer goin'?

LEN. 'Ad enough.

HARRY. No different any other place.

LEN. I've heard it all before. (Pause.)

HARRY. Thought yer'd like t' say good night.

LEN. Yeh. Ta.

HARRY. They're all in bed.

LEN. I get in the way, don't I?

HARRY. Take no notice.

LEN. Sick a rows.

HARRY. They've 'ad their say. They'll keep quiet now.

LEN. I upset every –

HARRY. No different if yer go. They won't let yer drop.

LEN. Different for me. (He puts a shirt in the case.) I never put a finger on your ol' woman. I juss give 'er a 'and.

HARRY. I known 'er longer'n you.

LEN. She reckoned she was late.

HARRY. Ain' my worry.

LEN. But yer 'ad a row.

HARRY. She 'ad a row.

LEN. You shouted.

HARRY. It ain' like that.

LEN. I 'eard yer.

HARRY. It clears the air. Sometimes. It's finished. — You shouted. (Pause.)

LEN. I'll 'ave t' look for that key.

HARRY. I left 'er once.

LEN. You?

HARRY. I come back.

LEN. Why?

HARRY. I worked it out. Why should I soil me 'ands washin' an' cookin'? Let 'er do it. She'll find out.

LEN. Yer do yer own washin'.

HARRY. Eh?

LEN. An' cookin'.

HARRY. Ah, *now*. (Pause.)

LEN. I can do without the key. I ain' goin' far.

HARRY. Bin in the army?

LEN. No.

HARRY. Yer can see that. Know where yer goin'?

LEN. Someplace 'andy. For work.

HARRY. Round Fred?

LEN. No.

HARRY. She won't see 'im again.

LEN. Best thing, too. Yer ain' seen what it done t' 'im. 'E's like a kid. 'E'll finish up like some ol' lag, or an' ol' soak. Bound to. An' soon. Yer'll see. (He moves the case along the bed.) That'll keep till t'morrow.

HARRY. It's a shame.

LEN. Too tired t'night. Wass a shame?

HARRY. Yer stood all the rows. Now it'll settle down an' yer —

LEN. I 'ad my last row, I know that.

HARRY. Sit 'ere.

LEN (sits on the bed). It's bin a 'ard day.

HARRY. Finished now. (A long pause.)

LEN. I'd like t' get up t'morrow mornin' and clear right out. There's nothin' t' keep me 'ere. What do I get out a it? Jack it in. Emigrate.

HARRY. Yer're too young t' emigrate. Do that when yer past fifty.

LEN. I don't give a damn if they don't talk, but they don't even listen t' yer. Why the 'ell should I bother about 'er?

HARRY. It's juss a rough patch. We 'ad t' sort ourselves out when you joined us. But yer fit in now. It'll settle down.

LEN. No one tells yer anything really. (Slight pause.) Was she all right?

HARRY. Eh?

LEN. In bed.

HARRY. Yer know.

LEN. No.

HARRY. Up t' the man.

LEN. Yeh?

HARRY. I 'ad the best.

LEN. Go on.

HARRY (quietly). I 'ad 'er squealing like a pig.

LEN. Yeh.

HARRY. There was a little boy first.

LEN. In the war.

HARRY. Then the girl.

LEN. On leave.

HARRY. An' back t' the front.

LEN. Go on.

HARRY. I saw the lot.

LEN. What was it like?

HARRY. War? (Slight pause.) Most I remember the peace an' quiet. Once or twice the 'ole lot blew up. Not more. Then it went quiet. Everythin' still. Yer don't get it that quiet now.

LEN. Not 'ere.

HARRY. Nowhere.

LEN. Kill anyone?

HARRY. Must 'ave. Yer never saw the bleeders, 'ceptin' prisoners or dead. Well, I did once. I was in a room. Some bloke stood up in the door. Lost, I expect. I shot 'im. 'E fell down. Like a coat fallin' off a 'anger, I always say. Not a word. (Pause.) Yer never killed yer man. Yer missed that. Gives yer a sense a perspective. I was one a the lucky ones. (Pause.)

LEN. 'Oo tied your 'ead?

HARRY. I managed. I never arst them.

LEN. I'm good at that.

HARRY. No need. (Pause.) Nigh on midnight.

LEN. Gone. (He takes off his shoes and stands. He drops his trousers.)

HARRY. Yer don't wan'a go.

LEN. Eh?

HARRY. Don't go. No point.

LEN (his trousers around his ankles). Why?

HARRY. Yer'd come back.

LEN. No use sayin' anythin' t'night —

HARRY. Don't let 'em push yer out.

LEN. Depends 'ow I feel in the mornin'. (He sits on the bed and pulls off his trousers.)

HARRY. Choose yer own time. Not when it suits them.

LEN. I don't know anythin' t'night.

HARRY. I'd like yer t' stay. If yer can see yer way to.

LEN. Why?

HARRY (after a slight pause). I ain' stayin'.

LEN. What?

HARRY. Not always.

LEN. Oh, yeh. (He puts the case on the floor.)

HARRY. Yer'll see. If I was t' go now she'd be laughin'. She'd soon 'ave someone in my bed. She knows 'ow t' be'ave when she likes. An' cook.

LEN. Yeh, yeh. (He slides the case under the bed and sits on the bed.)

HARRY. I'll go when I'm ready. When she's on 'er pension. She won't get no one after 'er then. I'll be *out*. Then see 'ow she copes.

LEN. Ain' worth it, pop.

HARRY. It's only right. When someone carries on like 'er, they 'ave t' pay for it. People can't get away with murder. What'd 'appen then?

LEN. Don't arst me.

HARRY. She thinks she's on top. I'll 'ave t' fall back a bit — buy a few things an' stay in me room more. I can wait.

LEN. 'Ead still 'urt?

HARRY. She'll find out.

LEN. I can let yer 'ave some aspirins.

HARRY. Eh?

LEN. Can yer move up. (HARRY stands.) No, I didn't mean that.

HARRY. Yer should be in bed. We don't wan'a waste the light.

LEN. I won't let on what yer said.

HARRY. Eh?

LEN. You leavin'.

HARRY. She knows.

LEN. Yer told 'er?

HARRY. We don't 'ave secrets. They make trouble. (He goes to the door.) Don't speak to 'em at all. It saves a lot a misunderstandin'.

LEN. Oh.

HARRY. Yer'll be all right in the mornin'.

LEN. No work t'night?

HARRY. Saturday.

LEN. I forgot.

HARRY. Night.

LEN. Funny we never talked before.

HARRY. They listen all the time.

LEN. Will yer come up next Saturday night?

HARRY. No, no. Cause trouble. They won't stand for it.

LEN. I'd like t' tell 'er t' jump off once more.

HARRY. Sometime. Don't upset 'er. It ain' fair. Thass best all round.

LEN (looks around). It's like that.

HARRY. Listen!

LEN. What? (HARRY holds up his hand. Silence.) Still cryin'?

HARRY. She's gone quiet. (Silence.) There — she's movin'. (Silence.)

LEN. She's 'eard us.

HARRY. Best keep away, yer see. Good night.

LEN. But —

HARRY. Sh! (He holds up his hand again. They listen. Silence. Pause.) Good night.

LEN. 'Night. (HARRY goes.)

SCENE THIRTEEN

The living room. PAM sits on the couch. She reads the *Radio Times*. MARY takes things from the table and goes out. Pause. She comes back. She goes to the table. She collects the plates. She goes out. Pause. The door opens. HARRY comes in. He goes to the table and opens the drawer. He searches in it. PAM turns a page. MARY comes in. She goes to the table and picks up the last things on it. She goes out. Harry's jacket is draped on the back of the chair by the

table. He searches in the pockets. PAM turns a page. There
is a loud bang (offstage). Silence. HARRY turns to the table
and searches in the drawer. MARY comes in. She wipes the
table with a damp cloth. There is a loud bang (off). MARY
goes out. HARRY takes ink and envelope out of the drawer.
He puts them on the table. He sits on the chair. He feels
behind him and takes a pen from the inside pocket of his
jacket. He starts to fill in his football coupon. A short
silence. PAM quickly turns over two pages.

Immediately the door opens and LEN comes in. He carries
the chair that Harry tripped over and broke. He takes it down
right and sets it on the floor. He crouches. His head is below
the level of the seat. He looks under the chair. He turns it
upside down. He fiddles with the loose leg. MARY comes
in. She straightens the couch. She takes off her apron and
folds it neatly. She sits on the couch and pushes the apron
down the side of the couch. Silence. Stop. LEN turns the
chair upright. He still crouches. He rests his left wrist high
on the chair back and his right elbow on the chair seat. His
right hand hangs in space. His back is to the audience. His
head is sunk into his shoulders. He thinks for a moment.
PAM stands and goes to the door.

LEN. Fetch me 'ammer.

PAM goes out. HARRY writes. MARY sits. LEN presses
his hand on the seat and the chair wobbles. MARY takes
up the *Radio Times* and glances at the back page. HARRY
takes a small leather folder out of the inside pocket of his
jacket. He places the folder on the table. PAM comes in
and sits on the couch. LEN turns the chair upside down and
looks at it. MARY puts the *Radio Times* back on the couch.
She pats the pillow. PAM picks up the *Radio Times*. In one
connected movement LEN turns the chair upright and stands

to his full height. He has grasped the seat at diagonally opposite corners, so that the diagonal is parallel with the front of his body. He brings the chair sharply down so that the foot furthest from him strikes the floor first. It makes a loud bang. Still standing upright he turns the chair upside down and looks at the leg. He turns the chair upright and sets it down. He crouches. He places the flat of his palm on the seat. The chair still has a little wobble. PAM folds the *Radio Times* and puts it down.

HARRY takes a stamp from the folder. LEN sits on the chair and faces front. He puts his head between his knees to peer under the chair. HARRY licks the stamp and silently stamps the envelope. He reaches behind him and puts the folder and the spare coupon in the inside pocket of his jacket. LEN gets off the chair and crouches beside it. His back is to the audience. He bends over the chair so that his stomach or chest rests on the seat. He reaches down with his left hand and pulls the loose rear leg up into the socket. HARRY reaches behind him and puts his pen into the breast pocket of his jacket. He puts the ink in the table drawer. LEN slips his left arm around the back of the chair. His chest rests against the side edge of the seat. The fingers of his right hand touch the floor. His head lies sideways on the seat.

MARY sits. PAM sits. HARRY licks the flap on the envelope and closes it quietly. The curtain falls quickly.

DIRECTORS NOTES

DIRECTORS NOTES

DIRECTORS NOTES